People often ask me, "Andy, what do you do?" For years I've answered, "Real estate," leaving people to assume I'm an agent. The truth is much more complicated. The truth is I've never held a real estate license, but I've bought and sold almost 2,000 properties. The truth is I have the time and financial freedom people dream of. Want to know how? Read this book. This book is an easy-to-read, no-nonsense, step-by-step blueprint to building a real estate investing business that serves YOU! Get ready to have your paradigm shifted.

— **Andy McFarland, Real Estate Investor and Mentor, Owner of Enlight Homebuyers**

I wish this book had existed when I started my journey. Having done 500+ flips and wholesales myself over the years, I'm shocked at how well it summarizes the steps you need to take. It has the road map to getting started then creating a six-figure or even a seven-figure flipping and wholesaling business. If that's your goal, then this is a must read!

— **Arianne Lemire, Owner of Glast Heim Home Buyers LLC**

Bill Allen has created a masterpiece for the common man on how to wholesale and flip houses for profit. In *7 Figure Flipping Underground*, stories from real people—from a Filipino immigrant to a Navy pilot, Xerox salesperson to a recovered drug addict and high school dropout—come together to share the epic adventures of building wealth and a lifestyle business through real estate investing. There has never been a book in real estate that provides the kind of practical business insight combined with real people, real struggles, and the real joy that comes when you do the work prescribed here. You owe it to yourself to learn the tips, tricks, and secrets of building the kind of life you want.

— **Terry Burger, Owner of Nice Guys Buying Houses LLC**

Bill Allen is a true success story. His desire to succeed and be present for his family propel him every day in his business. That passion and desire for personal and professional success is contagious to everyone who knows him. With this book, he has not only laid out his path to success, he also answers all the questions people have when starting out or growing a real estate business, so that you can find your success.

7 Figure Flipping Underground addresses the issues real estate investors have and makes the process extremely understandable. The stories Bill draws upon to explain how this can be done make the whole process not only clear but also refreshingly relatable. Where many business books just pound theory into your head, *7 Figure Flipping Underground* takes the time to tell you stories and create an experience that makes the information much easier to understand and to ultimately apply.

If you've been sitting on the sidelines wanting to get into the real estate game, or you're already running a small real estate business and have no idea how to grow it profitably, this is the book you need to have in your hands. This is the kind of book that you will refer to consistently as you build your company and ultimately reach your goals!

— Mike Simmons, Owner of Return On Investments, Podcaster, JustStartRealEstate.com, Author of *Level Jumping*

This book and a little bit of action is everything you need to be successful in real estate. It shares inspiring stories and real-life scenarios, and is a proven model to show you how you can achieve your financial goals and dreams. This is the ultimate playbook for a beginner or an experienced real estate investor. This book will change your life.

— Tyler Jensen, Owner of Utah House Flip, Creator and Star of the 7-Day Flip

7 FIGURE FLIPPING UNDERGROUND

How expert real estate investors find hidden properties, negotiate the best deals, and build profitable business

Bill Allen

Copyright © 2021 by Bill Allen

All rights reserved. No part of this publication may be reproduced, distributed, or transmitted in any form or by any means, including photocopying, recording, or other electronic or mechanical methods, without the prior written permission of the publisher, except in the case of brief questions embodied in critical reviews and certain other noncommercial uses permitted by copyright law.

Yazvac Publishing

Print ISBN: 978-1-7358035-0-0

Cover Design by Eled Cernik
Interior Layout by Laura Howard

This book is dedicated to my father, William Hand Allen. Growing up, he was a powerful influence. Someone I could always look to for advice and mentorship, someone to model, someone to emulate, someone to strive to become. When I was a young boy, he was published in the World Book Encyclopedia. I immediately decided, "One day I am going to write a book just like my Dad!" Well Dad, here it is! I hope there will be more to come, with each dedicated to all the other mentors and family members who molded me into who I am today.

How to Get the Most Out of This Book

Important: Read This First...

Thank you for picking up this book! I'm really excited for you to read it. But before you begin, there's something you should know.

I've put together a digital "Flight Plan Handbook" that goes along with this book. This handbook is where you'll find exercises, action steps, links to resources, and some bonus training videos to take you deeper into the topics covered in the upcoming chapters.

You can download the handbook FREE at 7FFHandbook.com.

It's important that you get this BEFORE you start reading the book so that you can follow along with everything we've laid out for you.

Pull out your phone or your laptop and navigate to 7FFHandbook.com or scan the QR code below now!

Contents

Chapter 1: The Leap 9

Chapter 2: The Silent Transaction 13

Chapter 3: What's Stopping You? 19

Chapter 4: Find Your Why 31

Chapter 5: The Real Estate Ecosystem 37

Chapter 6: House Flipping Is Simple, Right? 55

Chapter 7: Choose Your Market 69

Chapter 8: Uncover The Hidden Deal 81

Chapter 9: Top Marketing Strategies 93

Chapter 10: Lead Intake Secrets 107

Chapter 11: Master Deal Analysis 113

Chapter 12: Expert Acquisitions 135

Chapter 13: Funding Sources 171

Chapter 14: Smart Renovations 187

Chapter 15: Pain-Free Dispositions 205

Chapter 16: Take The Leap 221

Bonus Chapter Goal Setting 231

Don't Go It Alone 237

Acknowledgements 241

About The Author 243

About 7 Figure Flipping 245

Chapter 1
The Leap

It was a hot September afternoon in the Philippines. A 16-year-old girl with jet-black hair walked along a crowded street somewhere near Manila, one of the world's most densely populated cities. You wouldn't have noticed her unless someone pointed her out. And back then, nobody would have.

A decade later, thousands of people would know her name.

But on that September afternoon, she was just another teenager in a busy coastal city in Southeast Asia. She didn't come from wealth but instead from a modest home. And although it was one filled with love and warmth, as a teenager, she already helped to pay the bills.

Her name was Arianne Lemire.

She was on her way to her uncle's computer shop, where she helped produce employee ID cards for local companies. Her dream was to someday earn $5 an hour.

It will take a long time to get there, she thought.

A bus pulled up to the curb. Yet she walked past with her head down, picking a path through the bystanders who poured in and out of shops along the street. She could take the bus, but the fare was 10 cents.

It had been nearly half an hour, with another mile to go before she would reach her uncle's shop. She didn't mind the walk. It was better to save her money. Her mother had taught her to "Do what's right, not what's convenient," and values like this had shaped her into a sensible, hard-working young woman.

She was quiet and introverted—not the kind of person you'd expect to see clawing her way to the top of a Fortune 500 company or hustling to launch the next hot start-up.

But Arianne knew that if she did what was right and worked hard, life would go well for her and for her family. The future would be bright.

If she could only figure out how to earn $5 an hour.

Today, at only age 27, she and her husband Chris own nearly 1,000 rental units in the US, which earn $10,000 in net income every month. They flip and wholesale 100+ single-family houses every year. They live in a beautiful home on the Gulf Coast of Florida. And Arianne, once a shy teenager from Manila, is now at the helm of one of the most successful owner-operated real estate investing companies in the nation.

~~~

So what happened? How did Arianne and Chris take this massive leap from ordinary to extraordinary?

This book holds the secret to their success.

But this book isn't about Arianne. It's not about Chris either. And it's definitely not about *me*…not really.

This is about YOUR story. More specifically, this could be the next chapter of your life.

That is if you clear away distractions, focus on what I'm going to show you, read with an open mind, and apply what you learn.

I want to help you do four things.

- Determine whether real estate investing is RIGHT for you.

  Real estate investing is an incredible opportunity, but

that doesn't mean it's right for you. You might not be ready to fully commit. You might realize that you prefer the stability of your 9-to-5 job. That's okay. My goal is for you to come away from this book knowing whether you want to take the next step (or not).

- **Cultivate the right MINDSET for success.**

    You have the potential to design your future. You can decide how much money you make, how many hours you work, and how you impact your loved ones and your community. But you can only achieve what you want to. And you have to truly want it. More than that, you must *believe* it's possible. By the time you finish this book, you'll have the motivation and the mindset to succeed.

- Learn industry SECRETS so you can find consistent, profitable real estate deals.

    There's a ton of info out there about how to flip houses or make money in real estate. Unfortunately not all of it is good. This book is an insider's guide that will outline what's working in my business and for the hundreds of real estate investors in my 7 Figure Flipping mastermind groups—including how we're finding and closing profitable deals month after month.

- Take your first step (or the next one).

    Whether you're a completely new investor or you've been doing deals for a while and are looking for what comes next, this book is your one-way ticket into the underground world of off-market real estate investing.

It's one-way because once you understand this stuff, you'll never look at real estate the same way again.

We're going to break through the surface-level world of agents, MLS listings, and bank financing, and dive into the real behind-the-scenes strategies that serious investors are using to flip and wholesale hundreds of houses per year in cities and counties across the nation…without using their own money.

Nothing in this book is complex or hard to understand. It's remarkably simple once you see how the pieces fit together.

I'm going to take you through a process. The same one Arianne and Chris followed to retire in their twenties. It's the method I followed to build a multimillion-dollar company that ranked number 206 on the 2020 Inc. 500 list.

My company closes hundreds of real estate deals per year while I work less than two hours per week.

You can do this too.

If it sounds impossible or too good to be true, I get it. I felt the same way when I started in this business. Just keep reading. We're about to go *underground*…

Chapter 2
The Silent Transaction

While Arianne was walking to work in the Philippines, something was happening on the other side of the Pacific Ocean. A young Navy pilot stationed in San Diego was training to run a marathon.

That guy was me, Bill Allen.

I had played college soccer and was in good shape, but long-distance running wasn't exactly my thing. (And I certainly wasn't in *that* kind of shape.)

The marathon would take place in Ireland. It was a charity run—one of those events where the runners could get their friends and family members to donate money for every mile they finished. This run would support the Leukemia & Lymphoma Society.

I had commitments for more than $15,000 in donations if I made it to the finish line.

No matter what it took, I was going to make it.

I requested leave, and my commanding officer approved the time off. I trained for five months. Leading up to the marathon, I ran 40 miles per week. I bought my plane ticket and made hotel reservations in Ireland.

I was ready. I was determined.

Then something happened. A word came down the chain of command.

DEPLOYMENT.

I checked the calendar. Sure enough, the workups for my next deployment were scheduled to carry right through the marathon.

I couldn't believe it. All my training, all the donors I had rounded up…none of it mattered now.

Don't get me wrong—I was proud to have the opportunity to deploy and serve my country. I wouldn't trade my 15 years of active duty in the Navy for anything. But there were moments I wished I could live life on my own terms.

There were times I imagined what it would be like to have the freedom to do *what* I wanted, *when* I wanted.

But that's not how it works in the military.

As I canceled my marathon reservations, broke the news to my friends and relatives, and prepared to ship out, I understood that I was making a transaction. I had taken an oath to defend the Constitution, but more than that, I had agreed to lay down my freedom of choice in the name of service.

The thing is, we all make this same transaction every day.

That 9-to-5 job you're working right now—that's a transaction. You've agreed to give up your free time and cap your income in exchange for the security of working for someone else. You accepted the salary they offered. You work hard every day to earn it. If you stop working, you get fired. Those are the terms of the deal.

But the *real* transaction is even bigger than that.

How many of your kids' sports games have you missed? How many school recitals? How many romantic evenings with your significant other didn't happen because you had to work late? Or because you were too exhausted at the end of the day to put in the effort? How many trips, moments with your family, and life's beautiful twists and turns never happened because work got in the way?

We don't just trade time for dollars; we trade *our lives* for dollars.

And most of us don't even realize this silent transaction is happening.

My shipmate Neil watched the birth of his first baby over Skype. That's the kind of sacrifice the Navy requires. Neil is a great guy—he was proud to serve his country and he knew what he was getting into when he signed up. But in that moment, as his wife gave birth to their first child, the distance hurt.

Are you watching your life pass by from a distance?

What if you could work just a few hours per week—from anywhere, at any time, and without having to answer to anyone but yourself? All this, and you could bring in more than enough money to provide for your family and your loved ones.

What would that be like?

What would it mean to retire before you turn 40? Or even before you turn 30?

How would it feel to leave a thriving multimillion-dollar real estate business to your kids?

How would you like to be a force for good in the world? What if you could set an example for your grandchildren or be a positive influence in your community or donate $100,000 to your favorite charity?

Financial freedom, time freedom, and the opportunity to impact the lives of others—anything is possible when you take control of your destiny.

Got the picture in your mind?

Now I want you to understand something crucial.

At this moment, tens of thousands of people just like you are *living* that picture. It's real for them. They're doing all the things I listed above.

And a lot of those people got there through real estate investing.

You can get there too.

I'm still in the Navy Reserve, and I get to fly for them part-time—but only when I'm available and it fits into my schedule. I take my family on vacation whenever I want. One of my favorite places to visit with my wife and three sons is Disney World. When we go, I tell my team I'm unplugging for the week, and that's exactly what I do. I turn off my phone at the airport and leave it off until we land back in Nashville.

I choose how many hours I work, what time I start each day, and what time I stop. I don't work because I have to; I work because I *want* to.

And I want this same freedom for you.

Who's Bill Allen?

I'm a real estate investor. But you probably already guessed that much.

In 2014, I bought a rental property. It wasn't move-in ready, so I did most of the repairs myself. I ended up selling it for a profit six months later. Since then, I've built a multimillion-dollar wholesaling and house-flipping company from the ground up. I hired a team, systematized each step of the wholesaling process, and grew it to nearly 200 deals per year.

The company I created, Blackjack Real Estate, has changed my life.

Now I get to change the lives of others through another company I run called 7 Figure Flipping.

I only work about two hours per week at Blackjack Real Estate. A lot of my free time is spent leading the 7 Figure Flipping mentoring and mastermind groups, where hundreds of real estate investors come together to learn, share what's working, encourage each other, and grow their businesses *together*.

I wrote this book for investors who want to follow this same path.

But we'll get to that later.

Like I said, this book isn't about me—it's about you.

So let's talk about you.

Chapter 3
What's Stopping You?

What's stopping you from making all the money you want flipping and wholesaling houses right now?

When I ask this question, I usually get one of three responses:

- "I don't know *how* to do it."
- "I don't have the *money* to do it."
- "I don't have the *time* to do it."

The good news is that you can overcome all of these issues.

But before I tackle them, we need to talk about your limiting beliefs.

STOP! We're entering the land of motivation. What's that got to do with real estate?

Hang on. Let me explain.

Limiting Beliefs

When I bought my first rental property, I didn't have a plan. I decided I would pick up a few rental houses from time to time while working for the Navy and earn a little passive income. I figured once I got to 10 rental houses, I could retire from the military after 20 years and be set for life.

I never imagined I would leave the Navy and start flipping and wholesaling houses full-time. I never imagined it because I didn't know that was a thing people did. I thought the house-flipping world was just fake TV shows, scammers selling courses, and DIYers getting lucky.

At that time, if you had said to me, "Bill, go make a million dollars flipping and wholesaling houses next year," I would have stared at you blankly and replied, "Huh? That's not possible."

And I would have been right. It wouldn't have been possible...because I didn't *believe* it was.

Our mindset determines our outcomes.

You literally cannot accomplish something that you believe is impossible. Your mindset and your beliefs have to change first. It doesn't work the other way around.

Because you're reading this book, you probably already know it's possible to make money flipping and wholesaling houses. That means you're already a few steps ahead of where I was when I started.

Read on for my advice on how to conquer the three most common limiting beliefs that I shared above.

"I don't know how to flip or wholesale houses."

It was sometime in December 2013, and my wife Lucy and I hadn't been on a date in five months. She was pregnant with our son Will, and a Ravens game was our first opportunity to get out of the house.

I was halfway through my first flip, so I thought we should check in on the project. I had arranged for drywall to be delivered and hung that day, so I asked Lucy, "Mind if we swing by the house?"

When we got to the property, my heart sank.

Nobody was there. No truck, no contractors...nothing. Instead, we saw 180 sheets of drywall stacked in the driveway. That's when I felt the first raindrop.

We spent our date night moving drywall in the rain instead of cheering on the Baltimore Ravens.

Back then, I thought the secret to real estate investing was obvious: buy a house at an auction, hire some contractors to fix it up, and collect the profit.

But it turns out this business is much more complicated than that.

I wrote this book for that guy moving drywall in the rain all those years ago. It's everything I wish I had known back then.

I'm not saying you'll be able to set this book down, snap your fingers, and instantly start making $100,000 per month.

But you'll have the roadmap. You'll have the steps. You'll know where to begin.

So if you feel like you're missing pieces, keep reading.

"I don't have money to invest in real estate."

Chad Lundell got drunk for the first time on his thirteenth birthday. He dropped out of high school his junior year. In his late twenties, he overdosed three times in one year. Professionally he was just barely keeping it together, while personally he was in a hole of depression with a serious addiction.

At his lowest point, he was out of money, out of alcohol, out of drugs, out of his home, and out of options. Chad spent his twenty-ninth birthday in rehab.

Years later, Chad found himself sitting on a Delta flight next to his landlord, who just happened to be Andy McFarland, on his way to a 7 Figure Flipping event. Andy spent the flight chatting with Chad and explaining the business of real estate.

In 2020, Chad joined my 7 Figure Runway program. He had been investing in real estate for about two years. Three days after joining, he got his first lead. Within just a few months, he closed four deals. Today he makes six figures a year, and his income is steadily increasing.

I'm telling Chad's story because he's an example of someone who had practically no money. He was in recovery without any resources. All he really had was sales experience and the time it takes to start a business (and obviously a ton of determination).

If Chad was able to go from spending his last five hundred bucks on rehab to being well on his way to a millionaire, what's your excuse?

"I don't have time to start a business."

Tanya Rooney is a project manager at a real estate firm in the St. Paul–Minneapolis area. She and her husband Matt flipped their first house in 2019. They both had full-time jobs and little free time. But they decided to do most of the renovation work themselves—plumbing, flooring, painting, electrical, and even some HVAC.

It was exhausting.

One morning, they were at the house painting interior walls when Matt got called into work unexpectedly. Tanya was left alone at the house, paint roller in hand, to finish the work.

While opening a can of Benjamin Moore, Tanya did a little math. She soon realized that doing a bit of work here and there after hours and on weekends was costing them more money in the long run. Why? Because of holding costs, or all the expenses that accumulate between the time you purchase the property and sell it.

She realized they didn't have *time* to do it all on their own. So she put down the paint roller, hopped onto Craigslist, and searched for painters. Within an hour, she had several bids.

Tanya and Matt ended up with a professionally painted house that was finished ahead of schedule because they realized their limits and leveraged others' expertise to get it done. The painters gained some income, the job was done right, and Tanya and Matt were able to spend what little free time they had on other things, like looking for their next house. Eventually she joined my 7 Figure Flipping Runway group, and soon after, quit her job to flip full-time.

Even if you don't have much time, you can still flip and wholesale houses.

You Need Time Or Money (But Not Both)

The good news is that you can make money investing in real estate even if you don't have your own money to invest at the start. And you can do it even if you don't have much free time.

But you need one or the other—time OR money.

If you have no time to work on your real estate business and no money to hire anyone to help, you'll need to make some adjustments elsewhere in your life before you can start making progress on your goals. And that's okay—we all have to start somewhere.

Think about how you can restructure things to free up the space for this new venture. Can you carve out three hours on Saturday afternoons? Can you cut something out of your monthly budget and start saving some capital? Find what works for you.

> The members of my 7 Figure Flipping mastermind groups learn how to do this regularly with one of our productivity coaches, Nina Ferraro. She helps them find time where there seems to be none from their point of view. Check out the Flight Plan Handbook to download one of the exercises we use to find time in what appears to be a jam-packed week. To get your handbook, navigate to 7FFHandbook.com.

A lack of experience, time, or money are only three examples of limiting beliefs. Most of us have many that shape our lives. Often we aren't even aware of them. Below is a list of some other limiting beliefs my clients have come to me with. For each one that sounds familiar, check the box on the left.

- ☐ "Nobody flips houses full-time."
- ☐ "I wasn't born into money like these other real estate investors."
- ☐ "I don't have rich parents to help me out, so I'm stuck."
- ☐ "Real estate investing is too risky."
- ☐ "You have to put in long hours to flip houses, and I don't have time for that."
- ☐ "Maybe you can make some money at first, but eventually you'll lose it."
- ☐ "You can't make more than $100,000 a year in real estate."
- ☐ "Wholesaling doesn't work anymore."
- ☐ "Nobody would sell their house off-market at a discount."

If you agree with any of these statements, don't worry. We've all wrestled with similar thoughts. But as you gain confidence as a new investor, many of these challenges will resolve themselves naturally. You'll gain that confidence through knowledge.

Your Biggest Questions Answered

Now that we've tackled some limiting beliefs, let's get a few of the common questions, myths, and misconceptions out of the way.

- Do I have to quit my job?

No, you don't. Even if you're working full-time or part-time right now, you can absolutely build your real estate investing business around your work hours. I did it while working 60 hours per week for the Navy. Countless other investors have started out flipping and wholesaling on the side, and some even choose to keep this business as a side hustle for years while enjoying the stability of their primary job. The choice is completely up to you.

- Do I need to work every weekend?

    It depends, but even if you work some weekends in the beginning, you won't have to do so forever. You'll need to set aside some time to work on your business, but that doesn't have to be weekends—and it doesn't have to be every weekend.

    I don't want to give you any illusions about easy money. The first few years will take some sacrifices. But as your business grows and your income increases, you'll be able to quit your day job, or hire a team and reduce your direct involvement in order to get your time back. Remember, the biggest benefit of real estate investing is that you get to shape the way your business runs, including how many hours you work.

- Do I have to know how to fix houses?

    Absolutely not. A lot of real estate investors start out feeling excited about turning distressed properties into beautiful homes, and many of them want to be involved in the process. That's fine. But you're running a real estate business, which means you need to focus on operating the business as a whole. Don't get hung up on individual houses.

    In many cases, the investors who genuinely love working on houses tend to stay in the contractor role longer than they should, rather than hiring the work out to focus on the higher-level aspects of the business.

- Do I need a real estate license?

  Nope, you don't. Legally, you do not need a real estate license to flip or wholesale houses. However, there are pros and cons to having one.

  The pros include being able to list houses yourself and collect the commission when they sell. Having a license makes it easier to get access to the Multiple Listing Service (MLS), which provides full details on properties that are either up for sale or have been sold on the open market. And you'll avoid scheduling and then waiting for a real estate agent to let you into a house. You may even learn a thing or two about the real estate market while studying for your license.

  As for the cons? Well, first off, you're going to have to invest some time into getting and maintaining your license. You're likely better off spending that time getting your next deal. And depending on the state you live in, once you have a license, you will typically have to disclose that you're an agent in certain cases when marketing to sellers, and you may be limited in some of the words you're legally allowed to use in your marketing. This varies a bit by location.

  The biggest con to having a license is that you may get distracted from your big-picture goal: becoming a successful real estate investor. It's tempting to save commissions by listing your houses yourself, but your time could be better spent elsewhere!

PROS	CONS
Commission from sale	Time and money to get license
Control over listing	Requirement to maintain license
Access to the MLS	Legal limitations in marketing
Convenience	Obligation to disclose status as agent
Knowledge about real estate investing	Distraction from running business

If the pros outweigh the cons for you, don't overthink it—just act! I got my Florida license early so I wouldn't have to wait for other people to open houses up for me and so I could get access to the MLS. But I got distracted and wasted a year listing houses and helping buyers, when I should have been putting that time and effort into my investing business.

- Do I have to live in a big city?

    The short answer is no. The longer answer is you can flip and wholesale houses just about anywhere—but there are pros and cons to doing so in big cities versus small towns and rural areas.

    In general, it's harder to find good deals in big cities, and the barriers to entry are often a bit higher. There's more competition from other investors and conventional buyers. The houses are often more expensive.

    But it's also usually easier to exit a deal in a big city. Whether you're flipping a house or wholesaling it, buyers are easier to find. That means your properties will spend less time sitting on the market, which means lower holding costs for you.

    Small cities and towns and rural areas are the opposite—fewer investors fighting over deals, but also fewer buyers.

    Whether you live in a small town or a big city, focus on the advantages of your situation and leverage your strengths.

- Do I have to be a "people person"?

    "What if I'm an introvert?"

    "What if I'm not good at networking and meeting people and negotiating?"

    "What if I don't have good social skills or confidence?"

    If some of these sound like you, don't worry. You're in good company.

For example, I hate talking on the phone. The first team member I hired was someone to take calls. That was pretty much the whole job description.

I know plenty of introverts (like Arianne and Chris) who have achieved incredible things in this business. And I know people who are naturally savvy and can't help being friends with everyone they meet who have gone on to achieve amazing results as well.

- Do I have to be a real estate expert?

    Nope. You don't need a degree in economics or finance. You don't have to be a sophisticated investor with years of experience trading in other asset classes or anything like that.

    I am a Navy pilot with an engineering degree. Actually, when I started, everyone told me that engineers make horrible real estate investors because they overanalyze everything. Not true!

    If you have a relevant degree or experience, great! If not, don't worry. Real estate is so powerful because it doesn't discriminate.

So what do you need to get started in real estate investing (REI)? Obviously, you need the key strategies and processes in this book that investors use to make money in real estate. But you also need to get started on your new business...today!

Pilots never leave for a mission without a flight plan. The same should be true of real estate investors. Throughout the rest of this book, look for the Flight Plan Handbook activities in each chapter. In fact, here's the first one.

**FLIGHT PLAN HANDBOOK:
Find Your Strength**

Everyone has a set of strengths—whether they are personality traits, skills, or special contacts—that they can leverage to give them an advantage. If you have time but not money, you'll be able to do things busy investors can't. If you have money but not time, you'll be able to move faster than a lot of other investors and make waves sooner.

Whatever your situation is, make the decision to see it as an opportunity instead of a problem. And then leverage your strengths.

What strengths do you possess that could help you succeed as a real estate investor? Check the boxes next to any statements below that are true for you.

- ☐ I have ample time to dedicate to a real estate business.
- ☐ I have the money to hire an excellent team.
- ☐ I have connections and know people in the industry such as brokers and lenders.
- ☐ I am a skilled salesperson with experience negotiating and closing deals.
- ☐ I have leadership experience.
- ☐ I am a real estate professional, like an appraiser or agent, with industry knowledge.
- ☐ I am good with numbers and accounting.
- ☐ I am a contractor who can walk into a house and assess rehab costs, create a materials list, and build out a scope of work with ease.

These are just a few examples. Think of any skills or connections or contacts you have. Figure out what makes you unique and how you can use your strengths to succeed in this business.

Now let's talk about what will fuel those strengths, or what I call your WHY.

Chapter 4
Find Your Why

In 2014, while I was taking my first stumbling steps into real estate, my wife Lucy and I were getting ready for the start of another new journey.

She was pregnant with our first son, Will. We couldn't wait to meet him.

I was spending early mornings, evenings, and weekends working on what would become my first flip. Lucy joined in to help with the renovations when she could. I have pictures of her, pregnant with Will, wearing a respirator while painting the basement walls. It was fun tackling this project together.

But I had a gnawing feeling in my gut. I knew we couldn't keep this up once our baby arrived.

As Lucy's due date approached, we found out that Will was breech, meaning he was positioned head up in the womb and aimed to come out feet first. Our obstetrician attempted to turn him around. The procedure, called an external cephalic version, ended up being much more involved and complicated than we had anticipated.

Shortly after they started trying to manipulate the baby's position, the nurse announced, "We have a problem."

Will's heart rate was dropping.

I'll never forget the dread and panic I felt in that moment. *This cannot be happening.*

The obstetrician turned to Lucy and me. "We need to get him out now. She needs an emergency C-section."

Although it wasn't what we had planned, the operation went well, and Will was delivered healthy and stable. Lucy was pretty much knocked out from a botched epidural and overall stress, so I was the first to hold him. Holding my newborn son in my arms, I was filled with overwhelming joy and excitement...combined with straight-up exhaustion.

But there was another thought at the back of my mind—a quiet but frightening one.

How am I going to support three people on my military salary and still reach my freedom goal?

I thought about what things had been like for me growing up and what my dad had gone through.

My dad had served in the U.S. Navy as an officer working on submarines in San Diego. He knew it would be challenging raising a family in the military, so not long after I was born, he left active duty and went into the reserves—the same path I would later take. Around the time I finished high school, his business took off. After that, he never missed another game or another dinner. My dad had created time and financial freedom for himself, but it had taken him 10 years to do it.

Holding Will at the hospital that first day after the emergency C-section, I knew I didn't want to do exactly what my dad had done. I wanted to be at *all* of Will's sports games—the whole time, not just in high school. I wanted to coach his teams.

I decided I would go all-in on this real estate thing. But I was going to figure out a way to do it without having to spend all my nights and weekends laying tile and installing toilets and scraping paint off walls.

I wanted more income. I wanted to provide for my growing family.

But more than that, I wanted *time*.

And my WHY? I was holding him in my arms.

It's More Than Just The Money

Most real estate investors get into this business to make money. That's what brought me here. But in the end, it's about more than just the money.

We're after something deeper.

And that's a good thing—if it were only about money, most of us would not succeed long-term.

After Will was born, I sat down with Lucy and told her about my dream of building a real estate business. I explained that it would take a lot of work and that I wouldn't be much help for the next year, but after that (assuming it worked), I'd be around a lot.

With her blessing, I dove in with a passion. I set my alarm for 5:00 AM each day to sneak in two hours of work before my family got up. I ate breakfast with them before heading to work to fly for the Navy. I got home around 6:00 PM, ate dinner with my family, played with Will for an hour, gave him a bath, read him a story, put him to bed, then worked another two to four hours in my home office. I spent every weekend running to appointments.

And I woke up to do it again the next day and the day after that. It took me four and a half months, $22,500 in expenses, and countless hours of hustle to get my first deal.

If money had been my only motivation, I would have turned around after month two or three. But I knew I was building something that would give me the freedom and stability I wanted for myself and my family. So I stuck with it.

Here's why this matters…

The #1 Reason Investors Fail

The biggest reason new real estate investors fail is because they only kind of want it. This business is easy to learn but tough to do. It takes hard work, repeated over months and years.

If you're only half in—meaning you're interested in doing it, but you could just as easily stop if you needed to—you will not succeed. I'm not trying to be harsh. But there will be discouraging moments. Maybe *more* than discouraging. You'll want to quit. You'll feel alone. You'll doubt yourself. You'll wonder whether you should cut your losses.

Mike Tyson said, "Everyone has a plan until they get punched in the mouth." Eventually something will land a punch. And one of your limiting beliefs will make it hard to get back up.

On those days, the *only* thing that will get you through to the other side is your WHY.

Why do you want this?

Your WHY needs to be rock solid. Undeniable. Impossible to ignore. You must be utterly, completely convinced that your WHY is worth doing just about anything for. If not—if your WHY is wishy-washy or uninspiring to you—you aren't going to make it.

My friend Adam Rae always says that you need to have both a selfish WHY and a selfless WHY. I agree, and I think this is a perfect way to look at it.

There's something you want for yourself—money, time, freedom. You've got to have this "selfish" thing as part of your WHY, or you'll end up feeling resentful. But wanting something for yourself isn't enough. What do you want for those you love? What do you want for others in your life?

Combine your selfish WHY and your selfless WHY, and you'll be ready to power through any obstacle you face.

> **FLIGHT PLAN HANDBOOK:**
> **Find Your WHYs**
>
> The only way to get clarity on this is to look deep inside and be brutally honest with yourself. What truly matters to you more than anything else? Here are a few examples of the powerful WHYs that drive me and my clients.
>
> - Send my kids to good colleges
> - Be there for my family in an instant whenever they need me
> - Pay for medical care for a loved one
> - Give my parents the retirement they deserve
> - Provide my kids with the childhood I wish I could have had
> - Travel around the world while my business runs itself
> - Donate to charity and impact the causes I support
> - Make my mark on the world and leave a legacy
> - Fulfill the mission or purpose of my life
>
> Your WHY is what will get you through the rough days. Don't rush this—take some time to nail it down.

Now that you have identified your motivation, it's time for you to learn the most critical, and misunderstood, element of underground real estate investing. It's not a trick or hack or tip, but instead the foundation of investment basics. If you wrap your head around the real estate ecosystem, you'll step into another world entirely.

Chapter 5
The Real Estate Ecosystem

Arianne stepped off a plane in Pensacola, Florida, with nothing but a suitcase and $50,000 of student debt. She soon found work as a speech pathologist and her husband Chris became a software engineer. They both made good money and, from the outside looking in, they had made it.

But there was a problem.

Arianne worked 60 or more hours a week. She loved the work she was doing and found it fulfilling and interesting, but she was the only speech pathologist in the building, which meant it was almost impossible to get time off.

It had been a long time since she had seen her family in New Zealand. And she hadn't been back to the Philippines to visit relatives in years.

Flights weren't cheap. Money was tight. But finding *time* was the biggest challenge.

Arianne felt trapped. She knew it might be years before she'd get to see her family again. And what if she and Chris had kids? Would their kids *ever* be able to meet their grandparents, cousins, uncles, and aunts? Or would they grow up as strangers, only connecting with family once or twice for the occasional expensive reunion?

They needed a way out of the day-to-day grind. So they started learning about passive income. One strategy came up again and again in their research: rental properties.

They saved their money, talked to agents, studied different areas, and eventually bought two rentals. The properties each brought in a couple hundred dollars in passive income each month.

Success…right?

But with their money tied up in those two properties, Arianne and Chris didn't have enough cash left to put 20% down on a third rental. So they started saving again.

This is going to take years, Arianne thought.

And she was right. Passive income from rentals wasn't going to solve their problem, not for a long time. They needed to find some other way to make money.

The Real Estate Ecosystem

There are a lot of ways to make money in real estate.

Flipping houses, wholesaling, landlording, wholetailing, new construction, short-term and vacation rentals, multifamily syndications, hotels and motels, commercial buildings, and land development are just a few of the ways you can create financial security through real estate.

Every strategy is a separate business model, but they all interconnect in what I call the **real estate ecosystem**. Just like in nature, each approach to REI has a specific role within a complex system. Soon I'll show you how everything fits together, but first I need to explain a fundamental truth about investing:

Not all tactics are created equal.

Some are easy to start. Others have greater long-term income potential. Some are riskier. In this book, I'll focus entirely on the two strategies I teach to my clients: house flipping and wholesaling. Why? Because these are both winning strategies that any eager new investor can adopt.

Arianne and Chris had chosen single-family rentals as their business model. Nothing wrong with that. After you buy a handful of properties and pay the mortgage, you could have a comfortable income. But how many down payments could you make today? Probably not more than one, right? With rentals, scalability will always be a challenge.

And Arianne didn't want to wait 10 years to see her family, so she and Chris needed a faster business model.

I met them in 2016, at a Real Estate Investor Association (REIA) meeting in Pensacola. I was stationed there at the time and had just started wholesaling houses. I wasn't mentoring anyone back then, but I had just joined a group of investors called 7 Figure Flipping.

Arianne and Chris told me their story. "We know real estate is the answer," Arianne said. "But we need to find a way to do *more* of it."

"Have you thought about wholesaling?" I inquired.

"What's that?" she asked.

Most people have heard of house flipping. But wholesaling is less well known, despite being the best strategy for new real estate investors.

How Wholesaling Works

If REI is an ecosystem, wholesalers are the species that provide nourishment for all the other life-forms. Wholesalers "feed" the rest of the real estate industry by producing low-cost investment opportunities. Essentially, a **wholesaler** is an investor who sources and finds discounted properties and supplies them to other buyers, like flippers and landlords, for a fee. Let me show you how this works.

Remember Andy McFarland, the guy Chad Lundell sat next to on that life-changing flight? He introduced me to wholesaling too. But Andy himself had figured it out by accident.

He had stumbled through a few flips and was in the middle of purchasing the third. It was going to be a big financial stretch, but Andy was nearly funded and he expected to close within the next few weeks. He had the house under contract and intended to renovate ASAP.

That's when his agent called to tell him something weird. "There's another investor who wants this house. And he's willing to pay you $4,000 for the contract."

Andy replied, "Four thousand just for the *contract*? How does that work?"

"You would transfer the contract to him, making *him* the buyer instead," the agent said. "It's called an assignment. In exchange, he'll pay you an extra four thousand on top."

"So I sell him the contract, and then he uses that to buy the house himself?"

"Yep. Pretty simple."

Andy thought about it. The house was a disaster, and he knew that meant more work for him, a longer timeline, and higher holding costs. And he was concerned about wrapping up too much money in what could turn out to be an expensive project. A quick, easy $4,000 payday sounded pretty appealing.

"Let's do it," he said.

Within a few days, the deal was complete and Andy made $4,000.

Do you see why wholesaling is such a great business model? As a wholesaler, you...

- Don't buy the house yourself
- Don't spend any money or time on repairs
- Don't acquire holding costs

All Andy did was sign a contract with the seller, who then assigned it to another investor.

In a typical wholesale deal, the wholesaler will get the house under contract for whatever amount they negotiate with the seller, say $70,000. Then the wholesaler will turn around and sell the contract to another investor for whatever amount they are able to get, maybe $90,000. The difference between those two prices is what the wholesaler keeps.

In this example, if the wholesaler assigns the contract at $90,000, they will get to keep $20,000 ($90,000 - $70,000 = $20,000). If the house is a good deal to the other investor at the agreed price, then everyone walks away happy. The seller gets the amount they need, the buyer gets a great deal on a house they wanted, and the wholesaler gets paid for the time and effort they spent to find the deal.

If this all seems confusing, think of other wholesale transactions you're familiar with. Consider supermarkets. A farmer grows the produce, a wholesaler distributes it to the supermarket, and the supermarket sells it to you.

Wholesale real estate can be an extremely lucrative business model. Today Andy is one of the top wholesalers in the nation. His team closes several hundred wholesale deals per year across multiple states. And they make a lot more than $4,000 on these deals. In most cases, their assignment fees are between $10,000 and $15,000 per house, sometimes as much as $50,000 and even $100,000.

I'm sure you have plenty of questions, so let's break down the art of wholesaling real estate into simple steps.

> **Step #1:** Find distress.
>
> **Step #2:** Calculate your maximum allowable offer (MAO).
>
> **Step #3:** Get the house under contract.
>
> **Step #4:** Find an investor buyer.
>
> **Step #5:** Close the deal.

Step #1: Find distress.

This is one of the most crucial steps in the wholesaling process, so I'm going to spend a lot of time on it.

I hear this question all the time:

"Why would a homeowner agree to sell their house at a discount below market value?"

The answer is *distress*. There are three types of distress in real estate.

- **Distressed Property:** This kind of distress occurs when the house or property itself is in bad shape. Think boarded-up windows, a collapsing roof, evidence of a recent fire or flood, visible mold, or any other kind of damage.
- **Distressed Seller:** When the homeowner is facing an issue or a crisis and needs to sell the property fast, you've got a distressed seller. Maybe someone in their family

recently passed away or they inherited an unwanted property. Maybe they are a tired landlord who is sick of dealing with problem tenants. Perhaps they can't make their mortgage payments or they owe back taxes. Sometimes a distressed seller is going through a stressful life event like a divorce or job relocation.

- **Combination:** In many cases, both types of distress will occur simultaneously. Imagine an out-of-state landlord whose tenants are trashing the place and missing their rent payments. Because of all the damage, the landlord would not be able to sell the house through a real estate agent without first making a ton of costly repairs.

When there's distress, sellers are often willing to give up some equity in exchange for a fast solution to the problem. They understand that if they had time to wait or money to make repairs, they could probably make more selling their house conventionally through a real estate agent. But they need an *immediate* solution. This is what makes wholesaling a win-win-win venture. Wholesalers help distressed homeowners sell their property fast, feed the overall real estate ecosystem with great deals, and earn income along the way.

But you might still be saying, "I don't know, Bill. I still think most sellers would just go the conventional route. These wholesale deals must be really rare."

Sometimes even if the seller wants to sell conventionally, they can't. If the property is extremely distressed, most real estate agents won't touch it. Agents earn a commission of about 3% on each house they sell. And because it takes just as much work to sell a house worth $30K as one worth $300K, they might decide that the $900 return won't cover their costs and time.

Also, buyers of these properties often can't get a loan due to the distressed condition. That means these transactions require a cash buyer such as a wholesaler.

On top of that, a beat-up $30K house will likely sit on the market for months, maybe even years. The agent can't wait that long and neither can the seller. In this situation, wholesalers like us can step in and solve the problem in a matter of weeks. We've done countless deals where the seller was literally in grateful tears because we were the only ones who would work with them. And these deals are far more common than you might think. They're everywhere.

A great wholesaler has a superpower. They understand what the seller needs, and they know that it's about more than just money. Frankly it has to be. Otherwise no one would sell below market value.

As a wholesaler, it's up to you to figure out how you can help the distressed sellers you encounter.

For example, we've paid for moving expenses and arranged and scheduled moving vans. Once we covered six months of mortgage payments during a renovation, while I personally drove to Wells Fargo every month to write the mortgage check.

We've had homeowners leave everything they own in the house, so we agreed to deliver their things to their new residence.

Another time, I put a down payment on a condo for a seller who needed to move immediately to be closer to her daughter.

Sellers need your help. Are you ready to step up and be the solution your market needs?

Step #2: Calculate your maximum allowable offer (MAO).

I'll break this down in more detail later, but for now, just understand that after you connect with a distressed seller or find a distressed property, you'll run the numbers and figure out what price you can offer while still leaving room for your profit *and* your buyer's future profit, which is called your maximum allowable offer (MAO). This is why the "distress discount" is so imperative.

Step #3: Get the house under contract.

You'll meet with the seller, build rapport, negotiate, agree on a price, decide how much earnest money to put in, and sign an assignable purchase agreement. This contract gives you "equitable interest" in the property. You then have the right to make money from the sale of that property. The best part? You haven't invested much into it—just your earnest money, which can be whatever you and the seller agree to. Sometimes we put down as little as $100.

This is the power of wholesaling, and it's why this is such a popular business model, especially for those just getting started in the real estate business!

Once the contract is signed, you'll double-check the paperwork, send your earnest money to your title company, open up escrow on the property, and assess whether a lien or mortgage must be paid off.

> You can download an assignable purchase agreement for FREE from your Flight Plan Handbook at 7FFHandbook.com.

Step #4: Find an investor buyer.

Your next step is to line up a buyer. This will usually be a house flipper or a landlord looking for their next deal. I'll cover buyers in detail later, but for now, know that you'll likely sell to another investor, rather than a first-time homebuyer. In wholesaling, the less time you hold on to the contract, the greater your return. Most homebuyers need a lot of help to navigate a home purchase, whereas investors can often buy a contract immediately. Plus they are less likely to back out of the deal.

Step #5: Close the deal.

There are two ways to close a wholesale deal.

- **Assign The Contract:** When you assign a contract, you come to the buyer with an assignable purchase agreement with the seller. This agreement transfers your equitable interest in the property to the buyer.

  We always do an assignment whenever possible because it's the cheapest way to close, requires none of our money, and is the most lucrative.

- **Arrange A Double Close:** When you double close, you purchase the property yourself. Then, whether it's a few hours later or the following day, you sell the house to the investor buyer. In this case, the buyer and the seller have no contact with each other, and neither side knows any details about the other (such as the buyer's final purchase price or your arrangement with the seller).

  This method can help keep the closing process smooth, but it requires you to have access to funds to purchase the house yourself. To make a double close possible, some transactional lenders will loan money for 24 hours. In other instances, you can use the buyer's money to close both transactions.

That's it. Just five simple components make up wholesaling. I'll break down each step in detail later, but right now I want to answer a question you might have:

Why are other investors willing to pay an extra $4,000 or $10,000 or even $50,000 to acquire these properties? Why can't they just find the houses on their own and save all that money?

Here are three reasons that other investors love wholesalers.

- **Wholesalers work OFF-MARKET to find sellers.**

    The contracts that wholesalers find and assign to other investors are *not* listed for sale on the MLS or through a real estate agent, meaning they are **off-market deals**. They uncover these deals by negotiating **direct-to-seller**, meaning they market to homeowners without an intermediary. Simply put, investors work with wholesalers because they find deals they otherwise couldn't.

- **Wholesalers invest RESOURCES to locate deals.**

    It takes a lot of hard work and time to locate sellers, establish rapport, negotiate a price, and get properties under contract. That's why wholesalers allocate most of their resources (like time, money, and employees) to finding the right property. As a result, they're fantastic at snatching up contracts that other investors would miss.

- **Wholesalers provide a SERVICE to other investors.**

    Other investors understand that wholesalers provide a much-needed service that they do not have the time or resources to do themselves. These investors (like flippers and landlords) spend most of their time and money overseeing renovations, managing contractors, acquiring funding, finding tenants, and managing the property. Therefore, the investor who buys the contract should be focusing on their business and not sourcing deals full-time like a wholesaler does.

These wholesale transactions are the foundation of the real estate ecosystem. Wholesalers find distressed properties, get them under contract at a discounted price, then turn around and feed those properties to other real estate investors (like house flippers and landlords). Therefore, the entire ecosystem depends on wholesalers using their resources to find good deals. Wholesalers supply the inventory for all the various investment models.

In my wholesaling business, we spend hundreds of thousands of dollars every year to find deals. Because the homes are discounted below market value, we don't have to negotiate terms with our buyers. They show up knowing they will be offered a discounted property, and they don't mind us taking our cut because they understand the huge amount of money, time, and resources invested in finding them. They want us to continue finding deals on their behalf, so they're happy that we're making money too.

The more money a wholesaler makes, the more likely it is that their business will be successful, and the more inventory they will provide to the marketplace.

In return, the flipper, landlord, or other investor takes care of the wholesaler by showing up on time, coming to the table with funding already secured, signing the dotted line without raising issues, and not backing out of the deal. If any investors cause problems for us, we don't offer them future deals— instead, we find better investors to work with.

As I've said, this business is easy to learn but hard to do. Luckily for you, I've learned a lot from the mistakes I've made along the way. If you think wholesaling might be right for you, consider how you can avoid these as you read about each one.

What I Wish I Had Known: Wholesaling Mistakes

As with any business, there are things that can go wrong when wholesaling. Here are a few lessons I've learned.

Don't go too broad with your marketing.

You'll learn more about marketing in the Finding Deals chapter, but for now just be aware that if you try to send a direct mail postcard to every house in your target zip code, you'll run out of money fast. That's just one example of broad marketing that isn't worth the cost. Your marketing needs to be targeted so you're getting in front of the most motivated sellers.

Don't stop marketing too soon.

I see this happen all the time with new wholesalers. They start running a marketing campaign to find motivated sellers, and after a month they haven't gotten a deal. So they quit. The thing is, we've found that sellers need to hear from us multiple times, often over the course of several months, before they're ready to give us a call.

Remember my story from earlier? It took me four and a half months to get my first wholesale done! Most people would have quit way before that. So if the first couple months are slow, don't give up.

Don't assume a seller isn't motivated just because they're cold or hesitant on the phone.

This is a big one. When I was starting as a wholesaler, I didn't have much free time. So I only wanted to speak to the most motivated sellers. As a result, when someone called me, I tried to figure out within the first few minutes whether they were serious about selling or were just going to waste my time. I was pretty intense about this—if I got even a hint of pushback from a seller, I would politely end the conversation and move on.

Don't do this. I missed out on so many deals because I wasn't willing to engage and have honest, genuine conversations with these people who needed my help. Yes, you do need to gauge their motivation, but don't do it too quickly. Just let the conversation unfold. Sometimes the best deals come from sellers who don't seem all that interested at first.

Set the right expectations with the seller.

After you sign the contract, tell the seller what's going to happen next. Give them realistic timelines. If you know you'll need to bring a couple buyers to the property to check it out, make sure to tell the seller about this in advance. The last thing you want is for them to become confused or frustrated or to lose trust in you.

Don't make the due diligence period too short.

This can be tricky. You're telling the seller you can buy their house "fast" to help get them out of their distress, so you'll need to keep your contingency periods fairly short. But you'll also need to leave yourself enough time to find a buyer. There's no right or wrong strategy here, and there's no exact timeline you should follow. Just be careful not to make your due diligence period too short.

Don't just give the house to the first buyer who wants it.

If you're doing your job right, multiple buyers will be interested in each of your properties. Wait to get a couple offers from different buyers before making a decision. If you give the house to the first person who reaches out, you could be leaving money on the table.

Follow up with your leads.

It's great when a seller calls you and wants to sell their house right away. But in reality, many are going to need time to review their options, think it over, and make a decision. Some people might not be in enough distress to see the benefit of working with you yet. This means you need to get good at following up with your leads.

We get about 25% of our deals from follow-up. But some of those happen months or even years after the initial contact!

A Quick Note On Integrity

Wholesaling has one of the lowest barriers to entry of any investment strategy. You don't need a real estate license. You don't need to fund a down payment, renovations, or holding costs. You can start wholesaling with little or no money.

As a result, pretty much anyone can get into wholesaling.

That's both good and bad. It's good because it means there's nothing stopping *you*; it's bad because this industry has attracted some unscrupulous, scammy, desperate people hoping to make a quick buck by taking advantage of others' misfortune.

For example, some wholesalers will intentionally promise a high price when talking with sellers, knowing they won't actually be able to assign the contract at that amount. They'll string the seller along until they find a buyer. Then they'll say that they had to reduce the price due to some made-up reason. This leads to frustration for the seller, who's already in a distressed situation and needs to sell fast.

Other wholesalers will keep sellers in the dark or mislead them into thinking the wholesaler is the one who will be buying the property rather than assigning the contract to another investor, which leads to confusion and disappointment later on if the deal doesn't go through.

The bottom line is there are many ways to take advantage of people in this industry.

That's not what we're here to do. That's not how I run my business. It's not what I teach my 7 Figure Flipping members. Scummy wholesalers give all of us a bad name and make life harder for sellers and for the entire real estate ecosystem. They also don't last long—the dishonest ones end up drowning in complaints and lawsuits, or they get shunned by the rest of the investor community.

Don't be like that.

If you operate with integrity and openness, and if you focus on truly helping sellers any way you can, you'll make money and build a thriving, sustainable business for the long term.

Wholesaling can be a wonderful business model. After all, it's what I ultimately chose for myself. For the right person, wholesaling can be a path toward financial and time freedom. And when done with integrity, it can be a much-needed solution for a neighborhood.

You'll get to understand the nuances of wholesaling later in the book, but for now, consider your answer to this question:

Is wholesaling right for me?

> **FLIGHT PLAN HANDBOOK: ARE YOU A WHOLESALER?**
>
> Most successful wholesalers have a few strengths in common. Identifying yours will help you decide which business model is right for you. From the list below, check any traits that are true for you.
>
> ☐ I appreciate the importance of marketing to sellers and am willing to put much of my focus into finding distress.
>
> ☐ I am great at building rapport with sellers and connecting with them on a personal level.
>
> ☐ I am comfortable with sales and have strong negotiation skills, OR I intend to hire someone with this skill set.
>
> ☐ I can network and build lasting relationships with other investors and understand the importance of maintaining a good relationship with my buyers.
>
> ☐ I can manage a team.

Bookmark this page in your Handbook, as you'll come back to these answers soon!

If wholesaling doesn't sound like the right fit for you, I encourage you to explore the next chapter. House flipping is fast-paced, exciting, and rewarding work. Especially when you fortify yourself with a knock-out team. And if you're thinking that you already know the basics of flipping, I promise you that there is more to it than what you see on TV. Read on, because I have some surprises coming your way.

But even if you're convinced that you are destined to be a wholesaler, don't skip the next chapter!

For the real estate ecosystem to function, it isn't enough that everyone understands their own role. It's a system, remember? And this network only functions optimally if each member knows what everyone else is doing (and why they're doing it). Trust me, this chapter is as essential to future wholesalers as it is to flippers.

So let's find out how smart investors flip houses.

Chapter 6
House Flipping Is Simple, Right?

Most people think they understand how house flipping works. You buy a house that needs repairs, fix it up so it's beautiful again, sell it, and keep the profit...right?

Well, sort of. There's a little more to it than that.

The house-flipping TV shows and YouTube videos usually get two major things wrong.

MYTH #1: The house must be beautiful.

The idea that every flip should be transformed into the poshest home in the neighborhood is a common misconception. As a flipper, your goal is not to make a house beautiful necessarily; it is to renovate to the standard retail value of the surrounding homes. That doesn't always mean quartz countertops, bamboo flooring, and whirlpool tubs—especially if surrounding homes have laminate countertops and basic carpet.

If you begin your flips with the dream of turning old homes into luxurious modern masterpieces, your houses might end up more expensive than others in the area. That's a problem because it could take longer to find a buyer, if anyone buys it at all. The last thing you want to do is sink a ton of money and time into a house only to watch it sit on the market for months because it's too pricey for the neighborhood. I've made that mistake myself.

If you're getting into house flipping because you want to turn your Pinterest dream board into reality, this business may not be for you.

MYTH #2: You can purchase at market price.

Actually, you must buy at a discount—that is, if you want to make a profit. Contrary to conventional wisdom, your profit doesn't come from repairing the house. Yes, once the house is renovated, you'll be able to sell it for more than you paid, but the value added will usually equal the cost of repairs. To make a profit, you have to buy the house at a discount from the start. You can't pay full price for a house that you found on the MLS then flip it and expect to make money.

So what is flipping then? A **house flipper** is an investor who finds undervalued properties, purchases them at a discount, renovates them to force appreciations, and then sells them for their maximum value. In the upcoming chapters, you'll learn more about each of these steps. But for now, here's a quick overview to help you picture the process.

> **Step #1:** Find an undervalued property.
> **Step #2:** Run the numbers.
> **Step #3:** Fund the deal.
> **Step #4:** Renovate the property.
> **Step #5:** Sell for a profit.

Let's take a closer look at how this is done.

Step #1: Find an undervalued property.

As a house flipper, you can find undervalued properties in a few ways. You could market directly to sellers just like wholesalers do and look for distress and motivation.

Or you could buy houses...

- That wholesalers have already found and gotten under contract at a discount.
- At county foreclosure auctions or online auction websites.
- That are listed for sale on the MLS.

Depending on the state of the market, it can be rare to find undervalued properties listed on the MLS with agents. But in some markets and with the right system, you can find deals this way.

If you're new to house flipping, the simplest way to get started is to network with wholesalers in your area and buy from them. But be careful—do your due diligence. Don't assume the wholesaler's numbers are accurate. Be prepared to run your own numbers on the houses they bring to you.

As you become more experienced and you begin to systematize and streamline your flipping business, you'll have the capacity to start going direct-to-seller and finding deals the same way wholesalers do.

Step #2: Run the numbers.

Let's talk about profit again. Remember at the start of this section where I said your profit does *not* come from improving the house? Renovations are actually just a part of the exit strategy—you're fixing the house so you can sell it to a retail buyer.

That's the only reason you're renovating it at all. You're not fixing it up to create a profit margin.

So if you aren't renovating for a profit, how do you make money?

Your profit comes from the discount based on the initial distress of the property. In other words, *you make your money when you buy.*

We're going to dig into the numbers later, but for now, just remember that you must do your due diligence and run the numbers correctly if you want to make money flipping houses. Get this step wrong and you'll just break even—or possibly lose money—on every flip, no matter how nice the finished product is. I've seen it happen again and again.

The good news is that once you learn the formula, it's not hard to build a healthy profit margin into every house you buy right from the start.

Step #3: Fund the deal.

Funding is the biggest difference between flipping and wholesaling. Wholesalers don't really have to worry about funding (since they do not actually purchase the property), whereas flippers have to come up with the money to buy the house, cover holding costs, and complete renovations.

But what if you don't have $300,000 sitting in the bank?

Don't worry. You don't have to use your own money to flip houses. In fact, I teach my 7 Figure Flipping members how to raise millions of dollars of other people's money! Most house flippers aren't putting their own funds into their deals. (We'll dig into this in more detail later.)

Step #4: Renovate the property.

There are three basic ways to renovate a house.

- Hire a general contractor to oversee everything.
- Hire subcontractors and manage the project yourself.
- Do all the repair work on your own.

If you don't have much money, you might be tempted to do all the work yourself. But I don't recommend it. Here's why.

- It's going to take significantly longer than the other two methods, which means you'll pay more in holding costs.
- If you're not a skilled contractor, the end result may be less than professional. You might even need to hire a contractor to redo work later, which will eat up more time and money. And if the work is subpar, the house could sit on the market or go for a lower price.
- As a real estate investor, you have a business to run. And that business isn't construction. The more time you spend at the job site swinging a hammer, the less time you have to find your next deal, market to sellers, or line up additional funding. You will have a big to-do list, and construction is one of the few items someone else can manage.

If I've convinced you to stay away from the power tools, you might be wondering whether you should hire subcontractors (called subs for short) or a general contractor (you can call them the GC).

Both are good options. Hiring a GC will cost more, but this person will manage the project efficiently, allowing you more time to focus on other aspects of your business. Working with subs will save you some money but will require a lot of attention to manage.

Whichever option you choose, make sure to include the cost of labor and management into Step #2: Running the numbers.

So many people ask me how to find great contractors. Here's an amazing hack to ensure one is always a phone call away. Ask the good contractors who they like (and don't like) to work with. Soon you'll have a running list of people to hire or to avoid. If you keep it up, you'll have a list of four or five names for any job. Then you will never have to hunt down an electrician when one cancels.

That tip alone has saved me a ton of valuable time and money over the last three years, and it came straight from a 7 Figure Flipping member. (Thank you, Spencer!)

Step #5: Sell for a profit.

As a flipper, selling is the "easy" part. It might not be effortless, but it's fairly simple compared to wholesaling. While a wholesaler has to pound the pavement to drum up qualified investor–buyers, a flipper can sell the finished home to just about anyone.

Once the renovation is complete, you'll list the house for sale with a real estate agent. You'll need to pay the agent commission, which is around 5% or 6% (typically half goes to the seller's agent and half to the buyer's agent). Keep in mind that this is 100% negotiable and depends on the market as well as what the agent is willing to get paid for their efforts. From there, the agent will handle the rest while you move on to the next deal.

Simple enough, right? Like in wholesaling, each component of flipping is easy to understand. But of course, it takes hard work and dedication to earn success. Again, you can jump-start your business by learning from my mistakes.

What I Wish I Had Known: Flipping Mistakes

Here are a few suggestions to consider during your first few flips.

Don't over-improve the property.

As a flipper, your goal is to take a distressed house and turn it into a standard retail property. You might choose to add one or two cool upgrades to decrease the time it's on the market, but they shouldn't take too much time or money to implement. Consider a tile shower or a bright yellow door, not brand-new high-end appliances. When you're finished renovating, you want your home to stand out a *little* so it sells fast, but not so much that it costs significantly more than other houses in the area.

Past a certain point, dumping more money into the house to make it nicer won't increase your profit. You'll just end up with a more expensive house that will take longer to sell, costing you more in holding costs.

Your finished flip may not look like what you see on HGTV, but that's okay. It doesn't have to be beautiful; it just needs to be *profitable*.

Stay away from the high-end houses in your market.

Determining which houses qualify as high-end is completely market-dependent, meaning I can't just give you a price range to avoid. I typically define "high-end" as the top 10% of any market. These homes will likely have a higher square footage than the market average, be in the best locations, and be finished with expensive materials and amenities.

So why should you shy away from these beautiful homes? Because they are risky. Here are four ways the high-end market increases your risk.

- **Lower Demand**

    Like all commerce, real estate is about supply and demand. And similar to most industries, demand decreases when price increases. The highest-priced homes in any market will cost more than a first- or second-time homebuyer can afford. This means that you will have fewer showings and more time on market, both of which impact your profit. (Also, buyers can be a lot pickier when it comes to the houses at the top of your market.)

- **Costly Mistakes**

    With a high-end home, the numbers involved are bigger, meaning you can make a lot more but also could lose a lot more. This is a problem when you're starting out.

    Imagine you miscalculate your after repair value (ARV), which is a critical estimate, and have to drop the price of your finished flip by 5%. You won't lose much on a $250,000 house. But on a $2.5 million house, that same 5% drop could sink your business.

- **Longer Timeline**

    High-end homes often take longer to renovate because they're larger and more complex. They also take longer to sell, because fewer people are willing and able to buy them. As a result, you'll pay more holding costs during and after the renovation while the house sits on the market.

    But the real problem with this longer timeline is that you'll likely end up doing fewer deals overall, which increases your risk. You don't want to put all your eggs in one basket by relying on one deal to make your profit. Flipping a single house is actually riskier than flipping 20, because even if you lose money on a few, you'll still make a profit. But if you flip just one exceptionally expensive house...I think you can see where I'm going with this.

Instead of focusing all your effort on one high-end home, diversify your investment strategy across multiple houses to reduce risk.

- **No Backup Plan**

  There's no backup plan or exit strategy with a high-end home. Let's say you're flipping a house and the market drops, or your renovation goes way over budget. You realize you're going to lose money on the deal. What can you do? Well, if it's a house at or below the median home price in your market, you can typically rent it. But if it's a high-end house, this backup plan doesn't usually work. For various reasons, it's hard to cash-flow a high-end rental.

  There are exceptions, but as a new investor, it's safer to flip homes at or close to the median home price in your market.

To be clear, some flippers do find success in the high-end market. I just don't personally recommend it. Median-priced houses are typically easier to find, faster to renovate, quicker to sell, and less risky overall.

Think about what a first-time or second-time homebuyer is looking for. They are the ones who will live in the house, so make sure you design it with them in mind. And just in case they don't buy, run multiple scenarios and exit strategies on any house you plan to flip prior to purchasing it.

To determine a ballpark range to invest in, find the median home price in your area. Then calculate plus or minus 30% to 50% of the median. Let's say you're in a market with a median home price of $200K. In this case, I would recommend staying below $300K.

In the beginning, focus on properties close to the median. Once you familiarize yourself with your market, you'll have greater flexibility.

Don't fall in love with the property.

This might sound silly, but I see it happen to flippers all the time.

After six months of renovating, you might start to think a home is special. You may want to add some extra finishing touches to make it even better. You could become selective about who you want to sell to, or even refuse to let go of it for anything less than what you feel it's truly worth (through your rose-colored lenses).

But this is a business. Your feelings about the property shouldn't affect your judgement. Get in, renovate, get out, collect your profit. Then do it again with the next home.

Stage the finished home.

Staging is the process of making a property look homier by adding furnishings like couches, tables, and art. In the beginning, I didn't want to spend money on staging. But over time, I found that it was worth it. It warms up the home and helps the buyer imagine living there. It also draws the eye away from any imperfections. Today, we pay about 1% of the sale price to have our real estate agent stage the house for us, and we sell our houses faster and for more money because of it.

Lower your price quickly to sell.

If your flip isn't selling, try nudging your asking price down sooner rather than later. It hurts to watch your profit margin shrink, but you're going to keep paying holding costs each month your house sits on the market. And you'll likely lose a lot more if you don't adjust the pricing quickly enough.

Have multiple exit strategies.

I mentioned this in the high-end homes section, but it's so crucial I'll repeat it here. Always go into each project with multiple exit strategies. If you lower the price of a house and it still doesn't sell, you could potentially turn the property into a long-term or short-term rental. When the price of housing in the area increases, you can put it back on the market and sell for a profit.

Don't stop looking for your next deal.

Once you begin renovating a property, don't stop looking for the next deal. It took me a while to learn this lesson. I used to focus on one flip at a time, taking each house from start to finish before looking for the next one. It would then take me six months to find my next deal. As a result, I only flipped one house per year. I left a lot of money on the table by not thinking ahead.

While you're renovating your first flip, keep networking, marketing, and doing whatever it takes to lock up your next investment. And then the next. And the next. This is the path to 20, 50, or even 100+ flips per year.

Work with a real estate agent.

Some house flippers try to sell their finished flips on their own. I don't recommend it. Listing your flip "for sale by owner" instead of with an agent is a lot of work. You don't need to waste time scheduling showings; you need to sell as quickly as possible.

A good real estate agent changes everything. They earn every penny of the 3% to 6% commission they make on the deal. Don't be afraid to leverage their expertise (especially if you're a new investor), as they can help you navigate the sales process. Also make sure you find and work with a great agent, not just the cheapest one or a friend.

Flipping is a profitable business model, especially if you learn from my mistakes. Many members of 7 Figure Flipping build seven-figure businesses this way. But that doesn't necessarily mean it's right for you. The next activity will help you decide.

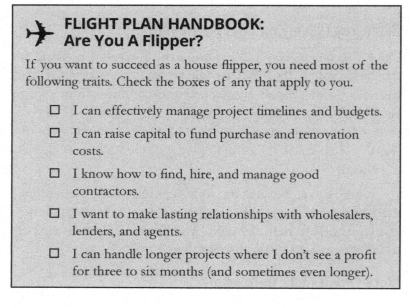

FLIGHT PLAN HANDBOOK: Are You A Flipper?

If you want to succeed as a house flipper, you need most of the following traits. Check the boxes of any that apply to you.

- ☐ I can effectively manage project timelines and budgets.
- ☐ I can raise capital to fund purchase and renovation costs.
- ☐ I know how to find, hire, and manage good contractors.
- ☐ I want to make lasting relationships with wholesalers, lenders, and agents.
- ☐ I can handle longer projects where I don't see a profit for three to six months (and sometimes even longer).

Compare the boxes you checked off on this list to the wholesaler list in the previous chapter. Which path is the right choice for you: flipping or wholesaling? If you're not sure, take some time and reflect on your strengths and your weaknesses.

If you like the idea of running marketing campaigns, meeting with sellers face-to-face, finding solutions to their problems, negotiating, and getting in and out of each deal quickly, wholesaling might be the way to go.

If you're more interested in project management, working with contractors, raising money, and improving homes and neighborhoods, flipping could be a better option.

Only you know the answer. And if you *don't* know yet, that's okay. Keep reading. We're going to dig into the details in the coming chapters. By the end, you'll be ready to make money with either business model.

No matter which you choose, one of the major decisions you'll make is the area to invest in. This is a topic with a lot of depth, and there are no black-and-white answers. With that in mind, up next is a guide to help you move in the right direction.

Chapter 7
Choose Your Market

After I speak at Flip Hacking LIVE each year, I have a strange, recurring conversation with investors. No matter the town, city, or state, it always goes exactly the same.

It starts with an attendee saying, "Great presentation! I loved it. It's too bad none of the stuff you talked about will work in *my* market."

The first time I heard this, I was confused. "Why do you say that?"

"I'm in New York. These strategies won't work there—the market is too expensive and too competitive."

Well, I've never invested in New York. It *could* be different.

The attendee continued, "If I was in a smaller market, I'm sure I could get all the deals I wanted."

This single encounter wasn't all that weird. Until a few minutes later, when another attendee approached. "Thanks for the tips, but they won't work in my market."

"Let me guess, your market is—"

"It's too small," the attendee said.

I replied, "Wait...too *small?*"

"Yeah, if I were in a market like New York or California, I'm sure these strategies would work great, but there just aren't any deals where I live."

Flippers and wholesalers fly from all over the country to join us at our three-day event to learn what the top real estate performers are doing in their businesses so they can hack the pros. But it never fails—the excuses run rampant when I ask why the attendees aren't doing more. And typically, it's the market.

If you think your market is bad, your mindset is actually the problem.

You can flip or wholesale houses pretty much anywhere. Every area has its own challenges, but opportunity is everywhere if you're willing to see it.

- In small, lagging markets, it's usually easier to find and buy discounted properties, but it's harder to sell them.
- In hot, established areas, it's hard to find good deals, but once you find one, you'll have no problem selling it.

What does this mean for you? You need to understand what type of market you're targeting. And you may need to adjust your target market to match your approach or your business model.

Below I break down how to analyze a geographic market so you can set yourself up for success.

Should I Invest In My Own Backyard?

If you can flip or wholesale houses anywhere, it makes sense to do it where you live, right? In your own backyard, so to speak.

Yes and no.

You can find deals pretty much anywhere. But the real question is whether you have the capital required to get it in your market. If you live in a major metro area, it will be expensive. And even if you can afford all the marketing it takes to get just one deal in a high-population area, that doesn't mean you will be able to do so consistently.

But if you live in the middle of nowhere, you might be able to snatch up literally every distressed property in your area, since there will be little or no competition from other investors. However, there may not be anyone interested in buying.

In short, even though you can do this anywhere, you should analyze a few factors to determine your optimal target market.

If you can, focus on the area where you live or where you already have experience. This could be your hometown, where you went to college, or somewhere you happen to have a lot of connections. There are many advantages to staying local. You're probably already familiar with real estate trends, such as the high-demand neighborhoods or whether more people are moving into the area. You may already know where to find distressed properties. You've probably even met a few real estate agents or contractors.

With that said, here are some steps to follow when analyzing a market.

> **Step #1:** Evaluate market size.
> **Step #2:** Analyze supply and demand.
> **Step #3:** Find your competitors.
> **Step #4:** Network with other investors.
> **Step #5:** Locate your neighborhood.

Step #1: Evaluate market size.

Start by knowing your numbers. Use a data-driven approach to market selection to determine what your projected return should be.

Start by analyzing the population or size of the market. For investing purposes, I define a **primary market** as a city of around one million people or more. A **secondary** or **submarket** is a city of less than 750,000 people, like Huntsville, Lexington, Bakersfield, and Gainesville.

Primary Market	Secondary Market
Chicago	Rockford
Nashville	Chattanooga
Los Angeles	Bakersfield

I've invested in both primary and secondary markets, and after years of analyzing the data, I've noticed a few trends.

Primary markets have a lot more competition. That means it costs more money and time to get an investment property under contract. However, it will also be easier to sell for higher profit margins quickly. Generally, primary markets take more capital and greater marketing effort.

In contrast, it's easier to find distressed properties in a secondary market, because there's less competition. However they will be harder to sell. For new investors, secondary markets are easier to break into, but you'll have to do more deals per year than you would in a prime market to reach the seven-figure-income mark.

Over the past few years, my numbers have aligned with a ratio of 3:1 when comparing primary markets to submarkets. In my experience, it costs three times more to find a deal in a primary market than a secondary one. But investors make three times as much on that property.

My advice? If you're new and you have a limited budget, focus on a secondary market near where you live.

Step #2: Analyze supply and demand.

Once you have a list of potential markets, analyze the supply and demand for each one. This is the most critical step when picking a market, so don't overlook it!

Look for demand before supply. Why? It doesn't matter how many distressed homes you find if there are no buyers. You need to know how many transactions take place per year to understand how much money is flowing into the area.

- Do other real estate investors and cash buyers pick up properties there?
- Does anyone else flip?
- If so, what specific neighborhoods and zip codes do they target?
- How many sold homes are non-owner occupied?
- Is the demand for investment properties high?
- Is the demand for retail homes high?

You might think that if no one invests near you, it's an opportunity to move into an untapped market. That might be true, but if there aren't any other investors actively buying in the area, there's probably a reason. Proceed with caution.

Alternatively, if an area is hot, active, and slammed with other investors, you'll have to compete with them. Surprisingly, this is exactly where you should buy. If other investors are there, you know there's a market for your product. (Don't worry, I'll show you how to snatch up deals in any market soon.)

Analyzing supply and demand can be tricky. It's also not a topic easily covered in one book. However, the ability to run a proper data analysis is critical to your success.

> To make it easy for you, I've put together a free training video that shows exactly how I evaluate an unfamiliar market. As a bonus, I also discuss the other half of the equation: supply. Find it in the Flight Plan Handbook at 7FFHandbook.com.

Step #3: Find your competitors.

Studying your competition is always smart, regardless of whether you are a novice or highly experienced. It's in your best interest to know what your competition is doing and, more importantly, what they *aren't* doing.

I want you to go ninja on this one. Ask yourself, "Where do other wholesalers and flippers hang out in person or online?" Below I've shared some tips and tricks I have used over the years to move into an area and take over, regardless of the competition.

🏠 **Tip 1:** Set your browser's location to the city you want to evaluate. Then search investor keywords like "sell your house fast in San Diego" or "we buy houses cash in Huntsville" to find out who ranks high on search engines and paid ads. As I go deeper in my analysis, I call these companies to see who answers (if anyone) and to investigate whether their process is dialed in.

- How quicky does someone answer?
- How do they respond to my questions?
- Do they use similar tactics as my lead intake team?

You can learn a lot by getting in touch with your competition.

I make it a point not to click on other investors' ads out of respect. As you'll soon understand, each click is expensive.

Instead, scroll down to find the same company within the search results.

🏠 **Tip 2:** Opt in to every wholesaler's buyers list. Pay attention to what happens next.

- How many deals are they sending out?
- Do they call or email you after signing up?
- Do they have a lot of testimonials from happy sellers or buyers on their websites?
- Do they even *have* websites?

Find out how sophisticated they are.

🏠 **Tip 3:** Check for local Real Estate Investor Association (REIA) meetings, which host local investors who want to learn more about real estate and want to network. You can learn a lot just by showing up.

- How many investors are there?
- How often do they meet?
- How many seem serious?

When I was considering moving into the Chattanooga market, the only REIA group I could find was about a dozen people meeting at a Chinese buffet restaurant. The buyer demand was there, but this was another strong indication that there was room for my company in the market.

🏠 **Tip 4:** Look for online communities where wholesalers and flippers hang out. At the time I wrote this book, some great places were Facebook groups, online forums, and Reddit threads, but there are countless others and of course they are likely to change and evolve. This is an awesome way to see who is in the market and understand what they are doing.

Step #4: Network with other investors.

Meet other real estate investors in the area. They know what zip codes are transacting and at what price point. You'd be surprised how willing people are to offer help and advice. Start with those REIA meetings I just mentioned.

You might be saying, "If I just reach out to another investor and ask for their most profitable zip codes, they're going to laugh and hang up the phone!" And you're probably right. You need to offer something in return, and it can't just be a cup of coffee.

So what can you offer the established, successful investors in your city to make it worth their while? Remember the real estate ecosystem. Instead of calling your direct competition, contact someone you want to work with in the future and offer them the opportunity to collaborate with you.

For example, if you're a flipper, call up wholesalers and say something like:

> Hey, I'm a real estate investor who buys properties to renovate, and I'm considering moving into your area. In the future, I'd like to buy deals from you, but first I need to get to know the area better.

This is an absolute gold mine! Not only will you get to know the area, you'll also have the opportunity to meet with a potential collaborator.

If you're a wholesaler, call up a flipper or landlord and say:

Hi, I'm a wholesaler who might enter your market. I'm ready to allocate a lot of capital to find great deals to sell to investors like you. Do you have time to educate me on the market? Maybe you could tell me where *you* would like to find deals.

And don't forget to network with agents, contractors, and other professionals in the area—they likely have some additional insights to share.

Step #5: Identify your farm area.

When you operate in a huge city like the ones I mentioned earlier (like Chicago, Nashville, or Los Angeles), you can't invest in the entire city. Rather you need to work within a focused and targeted area.

Your final task of market analysis is to narrow your target market down to a few specific neighborhoods or zip codes. Take everything you've learned so far, from your own analysis and from the other investors you've spoken with, and focus on a few key areas.

This will be known as your "farm area," or the location where you will focus your efforts on finding houses, buyers, contractors, and contacts. Like on a farm, these are the places that are most rich (in soil and resources) and will produce the best harvest.

This step will combine the demand side with the supply side. You will want to focus on the areas with the highest demand as well as the greatest supply. This is the sweet spot where you can do repeatable deals and achieve the volume you need to run a successful business.

If you're a flipper, look for areas that are desirable and affordable for first-time homebuyers. These neighborhoods should contain *some* distressed property, but not rows and rows of abandoned homes. On the flip side, the area shouldn't be so affluent that only the wealthy can buy. You want your finished product to get as many eyes on it as possible, and that is usually at or slightly below the median home price in that area.

If you're a wholesaler, look for areas with a high volume of flips and rentals, as well as distressed properties. This usually looks like blue-collar and working-class neighborhoods.

When I first started, one zip code in Pensacola had a lot of cash sales to investors and signs of distress. It wasn't a full-on war zone, but it was a low-income area with above-average crime. I was intimidated by the area and initially avoided it. In fact, it took me two years to market there. But now that we do, we make half of our income in all of Pensacola from that one zip code alone!

After you've done your research and identified your farm area, you're ready to find deals.

> **FLIGHT PLAN HANDBOOK:**
> **Identify Your Farm Area**
>
> It's time to identify your target market by working through the steps below.
>
> 1. Are you going to target a primary market or a secondary market? Choose two or three of each to evaluate.
> 2. Watch the training video at 7FFHandbook.com to learn how to analyze supply and demand.
> 3. Narrow your search down to a maximum of three markets.
> 4. Research competitors in the area.
> 5. Reduce your search to a single market.
> 6. Create a plan to network with other investors in that area.
> 7. Dial in your target zip codes for that market and finalize your farm area.
>
> Don't make the mistake of assuming you'll only have to do this once. As you grow your real estate business, you'll refine and expand your farm area. You may even move into different markets. Because you never want to limit your potential, take some time to really understand each metric and what it can tell you about a specific market.

Now you're all set for the next step—marketing to sellers!

Chapter 8
Uncover The Hidden Deal

I'll never forget the call we got from a young woman who said she needed to sell her house quickly because she "couldn't keep living with her mother."

My lead intake manager at the time Dee Dee had heard all kinds of wild stories. But nothing like this.

"She just won't leave," the young woman said. "She lives here but we want her out."

"Is she a tenant in the house?" Dee Dee asked.

"No. I mean yes...I guess? I don't know."

"Do you own the house?"

"No, I don't own it."

"So it's your mother's house?"

"What? No, she doesn't own it either."

This was getting weird. Dee Dee pressed on. "Who owns it?"

"My uncle owns the house. He said we could stay here."

Someone started yelling in the background. Dee Dee heard a crash.

The young woman sighed. "Ugh, there she goes again. She's out of her mind!"

"Is your uncle there right now?" Dee Dee asked. "Can I talk with him?"

"He's in prison."

Yikes...talk about a plot twist. Eventually, Dee Dee got the whole story.

The young woman and her mother were both living in the uncle's house. The uncle was in prison and wouldn't be out for a while. The young woman didn't want to live with her mother anymore, but neither of them had anywhere else to go, and the mother didn't want to move. The uncle had told the daughter she could sell the house and he would use the money to set her up somewhere else, but the mother wasn't having it. And it sounded like she was a violent, unreasonable person.

Can you sense the distress? Can you spot the motivation here?

No real estate agent would have taken on such a volatile listing. To make matters worse, the mother was a hoarder. The house needed to be fully cleaned out, and probably gutted, before new owners could move in.

Dee Dee set up an appointment for my acquisitions rep Eunice to go see the property. With all the issues going on there, Eunice arranged for a police escort. She met the police at a gas station around the corner from the house and they caravanned over to the appointment. When she got there, she took a look around and talked to the daughter briefly while the mother paced and fumed in the other room. After a short walk-through, Eunice made her way back outside, satisfied that they could make a deal—although it would require jumping through some hoops.

As Eunice headed back inside, she heard some arguing from the house. She turned around just in time to see the mother punch the daughter square in the face. The police officers grabbed her, handcuffed her, and took her away.

Eunice's next stop was to visit the uncle in prison to negotiate the price of the house and get the contract signed.

In the end, it all worked out. We assigned the contract to a landlord shortly afterwards. And the uncle and daughter were incredibly thankful that we solved the problem as a neutral third party, since neither of them could have managed it on their own.

I'm not saying you're going to find yourself in situations as extreme as this one, but sometimes when you buy houses from distressed sellers, you are called upon to solve complex problems. While it can be challenging, don't forget that managing distressed properties and owners is how we bring value to the marketplace.

So how do you find these distressed sellers in the first place? How did that young woman know to call us?

In this chapter, I'm going to show you how to dig up off-market, discounted houses.

Marketing Strategies For Wholesalers (That Flippers Need To Know Too)

By now, you understand that wholesalers find the deals and other investors simply buy from them.

So if you're a flipper, should you skip this section? Absolutely not.

First of all, even if you only intend to buy houses from wholesalers, you should understand how deals happen in the first place. If nothing else, it will help you understand why they charge a large assignment fee.

Second, many house flippers actually do find their own deals. There's no rule saying that flippers can't work directly with sellers. You can save a lot of money in wholesale fees by sourcing your own deals.

Keep in mind that when wholesalers negotiate with sellers, they have to set the price low enough that there's room for their own profit as well as the flipper's. There are many sellers who aren't distressed enough to agree to such a low price but who might still want to sell quickly at a discount—just not *that* much of a discount. By cutting out the wholesaler, house flippers can offer sellers a bit more money to get deals that wholesalers can't afford.

It's All About The List

Around 90% of your marketing success depends on your list.

In the beginning, this truth terrified me. I knew it was critical, but there was so much conflicting information out there that I got stuck in analysis paralysis. Basically, I just didn't have a list for a while. That mistake cost me an incalculable number of deals. So that you can avoid a similar fate, I'll tell you how to create and use the right list.

So what is a list anyway? In the context of real estate investor marketing, the **list** is a catalog of potential investment properties. Usually this information is purchased from an online vendor. It could include general data and information about homeowners and their properties. It could be addresses in a certain zip code, homeowners facing foreclosure, homes with recent utility shutoffs, or even the addresses of run-down homes you found in your market. And it could contain just 10 names or 100,000 or anything in between.

These are all examples of lists you can target with your marketing. And you can get access to them in all kinds of ways (including creating them yourself). For now, just understand that your marketing will be built on lists.

Start with a good one and you'll get leads and deals.

Start with a bad one and it could be like digging for needles in a haystack.

So what data should you use? And why does it matter? Without narrowing your search, you will waste a lot of time and money marketing to homeowners who aren't interested in working with you.

A *good* list is one that you've filtered down to include only homeowners who are most likely to be in distress, are motivated, and are ready to sell. For example, those who are currently in pre-foreclosure, meaning they're falling behind on their mortgage payments and the bank is preparing to foreclose, will probably contain a lot of motivated sellers. By contrast, a list of homeowners who bought their homes within the past 30 days will probably contain none at all.

Do you see why your success hinges on your list?

It takes practice to make good lists, but if you do, you'll have a big advantage over other investors.

> I've been pulling these lists for years, and I've learned what works and what doesn't the hard way—through trial and error. To save you time and a lot of money, I've put together a free training video showing exactly how I pull lists. I walk through which company to use, what filters to set, and what to watch out for.
>
> You can watch this training using the link found in the Flight Plan Handbook at 7FFHandbook.com.

Skip Tracing

Skip tracing is essentially the practice of locating contact information. This service is provided by multiple vendors online. Whatever vendor you use, the process is simple—you'll send the vendor the raw data (list) that you want to skip trace, they'll conduct a search, and you'll get back another list containing the expanded data they were able to find. Make sure that regardless of who you use, you only pay for the data you receive (which may be less than the total number of names on the list).

The output you get from online vendors will include all the data and filters you request along with the mailing addresses for each of the owners. What it won't include is the owners' phone numbers, email addresses, or other personal information you may need in order to market to them which is where skip tracing comes in. Additionally, after mailing to a particular homeowner the first time, you may find that some of the addresses are incorrect or outdated.

> You can skip trace to find contact information like...
> - Relatives
> - Vehicles owned
> - Cell phone numbers
> - Landline phone numbers
> - Driver's license number
> - Email addresses
> - Last known addresses
> - Age
> - Gender

In November of 2020, I used everything I had learned over the past seven years to help me buy the 13-acre property behind my house. I looked up the owner's name in the county records, then I wrote them a short letter explaining my interest in their property, including a little about me and my family.

But instead of mailing it, I went over to hand-deliver it. When I drove up, the owner was outside with his son fixing the fence. I was able to talk to him about the house, get to know him a little bit, and tell him what I was hoping to do. I left him with the letter and my contact information, and he said he would call within a week.

Three weeks passed and no phone call came. So I skip traced the owner and got his cell phone number and email address. I sent a quick text message to the phone number listed and BOOM—he responded within an hour! Three weeks later, my family owned his 13-acre farm.

Skip tracing can be incredibly useful, whether it's for a single purchase or to improve your bulk list. The more data you have, the better prepared you are to construct a multidimensional marketing approach. It's so fundamental to building good lists that my 7 Figure Flipping members get discounted access to skip tracing vendors (and bulk lists too).

Skip tracing also becomes essential as you pursue smaller, more targeted information like niche lists.

Niche Lists

If you want to get even more targeted with your marketing, or if you don't have the money to spend on bulk lists, you can use niche marketing to create niche lists. **Niche lists** include highly motivated homeowners found through diligent research.

Niche marketing usually takes more time, but the returns can be massive. You must be willing to put in the work—there's no way to shortcut the research by spending more money. As a result, it is something new investors can do that bigger companies often don't have the time or resources for. This means there will typically be less competition to deal with on these properties.

If you're new to real estate investing or you don't have much money, niche marketing can give you a competitive advantage.

Here are some examples of niche lists my team and I have targeted.

Delinquent Property Taxes

If a homeowner fails to pay their property taxes, the property can be claimed by the state and auctioned. Therefore, homeowners who are delinquent on their taxes may be extremely motivated to sell.

Many counties have online databases where you can view tax delinquencies. Others require you to request the list, which they will email to you. To view a list for your area, search the county name and the words "tax collector." Look for properties that have been unpaid for at least two years.

Some databases will also allow you to search for "estate." In these cases, the delinquent property is owned by an heir, who may not even realize they own it. If you can find the heir's contact info and make them aware of the tax issue and how you can help solve it, they'll likely be happy to let you buy the house. These leads are pure gold.

If you can't get to the property before it's sold, you could still get a deal when it goes to auction. Search "tax auction" for your target area to find more information.

Local County Court Records

Local county court records are another place you can find leads. Each county has its own system, but most are easy to navigate. One of the first records to look for are probates, or wills. Other records to search include civil circuit databases, which will show jail bonds, commercial foreclosures, mortgage foreclosures, and IRS liens.

In addition to the names of property owners, you'll also be able to find their current addresses, emails, and phone numbers. Sometimes you can even find a description of the property and financial information, like the mortgage amount, mortgage term, or interest rate.

If you're willing to spend some time going through court records, you can potentially find a lot of motivated homeowners.

Arrest Records

Homeowners who have recently been arrested often need to sell their homes quickly to make bond or to provide income for their families. To identify these individuals, you can cross-reference arrest records with the local county property appraiser website. You could also contact bail bondspersons or visit check-cashing sites and pawn shops. Those in distress usually talk to these folks a lot.

For Sale By Owner

As the name suggests, for sale by owner (FSBO) properties are not listed through real estate agents. With an FSBO, the homeowner wants to sell, but for some reason they're either unable or unwilling to do it the conventional way. This is a sign that there could be some distress involved, property or personal.

You can find FSBO properties through online listing sites like Zillow or Craigslist. Click the "for sale by owner" option when searching, or use it in the search terms. Sometimes you can even find landlords with distressed properties for rent who might be interested in selling on these same sites.

Water Shutoff Lists

Utility companies will shut off services in the event of nonpayment. This is a telltale sign of distress and typically the last bill a homeowner stops paying, as they need water and power. This list is more difficult to obtain but is extremely valuable. Remember, the harder you have to work to get information, the less likely it is that your competition is using the same data source.

Research your target area to find local water companies, and call them asking for this list. If they decline, call back the next day or ask to speak to their manager.

If you are still getting resistance, try sending the company a Freedom of Information Act (FOIA) request. This is a letter submitted to a federal agency asking for the public records on a topic. Be respectful and explain exactly what you are looking for. Not every company will comply, but it's worth your effort. This technique works on other utility companies as well, like electric, gas, and sewer. You can also search for utility liens on properties in your area. You are only limited by your creativity!

Garage And Estate Sales

Before selling a home, families will often have garage or yard sales. Find these sales in your target area online, and build a list of people who might be interested in selling. Try looking for estate sales on Craigslist or other online sale websites. These families are often motivated to sell their inherited properties quickly.

One of my first deals came from just walking into an estate sale and talking with the heirs who had recently inherited the house. You never know until you reach out.

If you're a new investor or if you're looking for low-cost ways to find more targeted, motivated sellers, tapping into niche lists is a great strategy. Of course, it isn't the only tactic worth considering. For example, the next one is old-school and reliable.

Driving For Dollars

Driving for dollars is the process of looking for distressed properties. Here are a few classic signs to look for.

- Boarded-up windows
- Long grass, damaged trees, or bad landscaping
- Garage doors off the rails
- No furniture inside
- No trash or recycling cans out on pickup day

When you find a distressed property, write down the address or use a map app to note the location. This is another way to create your own niche list for marketing.

Just like with the other lists I've mentioned, you can take these addresses and skip trace them to get the homeowners' contact info. Or you can just knock on the door or leave a note while you're at the property.

A lot of these homeowners receive frequent mail from investors. If the property is especially distressed, they may also have utility bills or a tax lien stacking up on the porch. You don't want your offer to get lost in the pile. If you leave a note, try to make it personal or unique in some way. And remember, it's illegal to place anything in someone's mailbox.

If you don't get a response at first, keep trying. Consider following up every 30 days until you're able to connect with the owner.

> **FLIGHT PLAN HANDBOOK:**
> **Make Your List**
>
> 1. Watch the list video (link in the Flight Plan Handbook).
> 2. Make a list for your farm area.
> 3. Design your list based on the filters below.
>   - Age of homeowner
>   - Amount of equity in the property
>   - Appraised value of the home
>   - Date the property was last sold
>   - Foreclosure and pre-foreclosure
>   - Geographic area
>   - Owner occupied or non-owner occupied
>   - Property info (square footage, bedrooms, bathrooms)
>   - Type of property (single family, multifamily, commercial)
>
> These are just a few of the parameters you can use to refine your list. There's almost no limit to the ways you can filter and combine the data. If you need additional inspiration, check out how other investors like you make their lists by joining my free Facebook group. The link to join can be found in the Flight Plan Handbook at 7FFHandbook.com.

Now that you've put all of this time and effort into a list, how do you actually turn it into a lead?

Marketing.

Chapter 9
Top Marketing Strategies

The most common way to market to these lists is through **direct mail**. This is the process of sending a letter, postcard, flyer, or other document to a homeowner that lets them know you're interested in buying their house. It also prompts them to contact you to learn more.

Direct mail can take multiple forms, and there's virtually no limit on how you can present your offer on the mailer itself. This has been a favorite marketing method among real estate investors for decades. And there's a reason for that.

Direct mail *works*.

You may have heard people say "direct mail is dead" because too many investors use it. Someone might have told you it's expensive compared to other marketing methods. Or perhaps you assume that homeowners completely ignore junk mail these days and won't even look at what you send.

In a way, this is all true—there *is* a lot of competition. Many people don't look at the mailers they receive. And direct mail does cost more than many other methods. We typically spend about $2,500 to get direct mail deals in our smaller submarkets.

But direct mail is also extremely consistent and reliable. It's predictable. And it's easy to automate. It's also incredibly scalable.

When I started marketing to sellers, I sent about 5,000 postcards a month. Today, we mail about 120,000 a month. As you grow and expand your business with new seller lists in new markets, your direct mail marketing can quickly and easily grow with you.

And your niche demographic probably *does* read every piece of mail they receive. Many distressed sellers are older, and like my grandma, they will read every sentence on every postcard and even keep them with their important documents...especially if we ask them to do so on the card (pro tip).

This is why, even in 2021, we *still* get approximately 70% of our deals from direct mail.

Don't buy in to the hype that direct mail doesn't work anymore. It may sound kind of boring and old-school, but it has been tested and proven again and again. If you understand how to use it, direct mail can be one of the most effective strategies in your marketing tool kit. But you must get good at it, test it, and be consistent for it to work well.

For direct mail marketing to be effective, three things need to happen.

- **There must be a clear call to action (CTA).**

    A **CTA** is a clear instruction that elicits a response. What do you want the person to *do* when they get your mailer? Again, there are multiple options—you could tell the person to visit your website, or ask them to call a number or fill out a form. And that CTA should be obvious and clear—not lost in a bunch of text or graphics. I typically ask people to call, so my lead intake team can immediately set up an appointment.

- **The mailing must be sent to the right person.**

    Direct mail is only as good as your list. Remember, the

most critical factor in your marketing success is *having a targeted list to begin with*. The smaller your budget, the more niche your list should be. This way, you can allocate your resources to the markets you know the best. If you have a large budget, you can cast a wider net and send mail to more leads.

- **That person must read it.**

    Your mailer is useless if no one reads it. This is why I prefer to mail postcards—the recipient doesn't have to open an envelope to view them. Even if they don't read the text, by the fourth or fifth time they receive a postcard, they'll start to notice my company logo. Postcards have the added benefit of being less expensive.

    Of course, you could go the other route of handwritten letters, which tend to be more intriguing to the recipient and as a result are more likely to get opened and read. They can also help build trust. If it takes too long to write the letters, go with a printed letter but pay your kids (or someone else's) to hand-address the envelopes. Choose an invitation-style envelope so it looks personal.

    Like I said, there are countless ways to tweak your mail strategy. Test a few out and see what works best for you.

Cold Calling/Texting/Ringless Voicemail

Cold calling, or making an unsolicited contact by phone, might sound intimidating. Some of the people you call will inevitably be annoyed and may even hang up. For this reason, many investors shy away from it. However, cold calling is a marketing strategy that anyone can do, making it a great choice for new investors.

Just like direct mail, cold calling starts with your list. It's especially effective when working with smaller niche lists. Start at the top and work your way down. In a spreadsheet, keep track of who you've called, when you called them, whether or not you left a voicemail, and any other helpful notes. You can pull a lot of deals out of small lists this way.

Calling isn't the only way to reach the homeowners on your list. Not everyone answers their phone when they get a call from an unknown number. But text messages have an incredible open rate. Instead of calling, send texts or build your own system around SMS marketing.

Ringless voicemail is another option. With this service, you can leave a recorded message on someone's phone without it ever ringing. Different companies will allow you to do this with either landlines or cell phones, and because the messages are sent out simultaneously to all contacts on your list, you can reach out to a lot of homebuyers at once without calling them one by one.

I'll finish this section with a note about the legal aspect of these techniques. However, to be clear, this is certainly not legal advice. Laws concerning marketing (especially when using people's phone numbers) seem to change frequently. Research your local laws, as they vary by state and even by city. As marketing evolves, so too will the different channels we use. Stay innovative, watch the return on your investment, and pivot when it's time to do so!

Internet Marketing

Ready to go beyond the list? There are a few marketing strategies you can use that don't require a list of potential sellers. One of them is pay-per-click internet marketing.

With **pay-per-click marketing**, you pay to run ads on search engines or websites such as Facebook, Instagram,

YouTube, or Google. These sites allow you to get pretty specific about who you're targeting. You can set your ads to appear when someone searches for a keyword like "sell my house fast" or "cash homebuyers" in your market.

The major advantage of pay-per-click ads is that unlike the other forms of marketing, the leads you get are people who are *actively looking for what you have to offer.* This is a big deal. Instead of you having to contact people on a list who may not be interested, motivated homeowners reach out to you.

The leads we get from internet marketing are often motivated, and the deals happens a lot faster than those that come in through other channels. We average about two or three deals per month through paid ads.

But they're not our cheapest deals. And they take work— you either have to pay someone to tweak the messaging and ensure each ad is converting or be willing to spend time learning how to do it yourself. You'll need to learn how to use various ad platforms and analyze conversion metrics. You will also need to get on these leads as quickly as possible, because if you don't answer your phone when they call, they will go to the next investor on their search list.

Keep in mind that laws are always changing on pay-per-click, and some limit the criteria you can use to locate interested sellers. Stay up-to-date on the best strategies.

When it all comes together, internet marketing is one of the best ways to quickly get motivated sellers into your pipeline without having to wade through hundreds of uninterested people. If you have money to spend but don't have a lot of time, this is a great way to go!

Bandit Signs

Ever see those signs next to the highway that say stuff like "We Buy Houses" or "Sell Your Home Fast"?

Those are called bandit signs, and they can be an effective way to get potential sellers to call you. If you're interested in this marketing method, I encourage you to leverage other people's time to set up the signs. It's one of those tasks that is easy to do but takes a lot of time, which means you should delegate it to someone on your team or hire someone to handle it.

Mike Simmons is a long-time house flipper and wholesaler, a member of 7 Figure Altitude, and on the board of directors here at 7 Figure Flipping. He has an inexpensive, automated system for putting up bandit signs. He orders the signs from an online company that prints and drop-ships them to a storage facility for a little over $2 per sign. The owner of the facility will sign for them and open up the unit for them to be dropped off. Then a local person Mike has hired will unlock the unit, grab the signs they need for that day, place them as directed, and send a photo with a geotag of each one using an app.

Mike pays the sign poster between $1 and $3 per sign. Once they have all been placed, he transfers the funds. With this system, all he has to do is order the signs, check the day after to make sure they were all put out, and make a payment.

A note of warning: Don't put your personal phone number or any other identifying information on the signs, or you'll likely get spam calls and even some complaints. Instead, set up a unique phone number that automatically goes to voicemail. You or a member of your team can check the voicemails throughout the day to see if anyone is interested in selling a house.

Make sure the automated voicemail message is clear and concise.

Mike suggests something like…

> Thank you for calling. We buy houses in any condition—fast, with cash. Please leave your name, phone number, and the full address of the house, and we will get back to you as soon as possible.

Keep it simple and short.

They are called bandit signs for a reason. Some municipalities have strict rules about signage, and will even fine investors for using them. Find out whether they are legal in your area, and abide by the local rules.

Networking

At my company Blackjack Real Estate, our marketing strategies are all about casting a wide net with tactics like direct mail and internet marketing. As a result, it's mostly an automated process that doesn't take up much of my team's time.

But if you don't have a big marketing budget, you can get deals for free without any real marketing efforts at all.

Since 2016, one of our 7 Figure Altitude members Sheri Duignan has been flipping houses in one of the most competitive markets in the nation—Orange County, California. When she talks to potential sellers, it's common for them to say something like, "I've gotten forty postcards from other investors just this month!"

Despite the high demand for real estate, Sheri flips about 12 houses per year. And she gets almost all of them by networking.

Here are a few ways you can use networking to find deals.

- **REIA Meetings**

    REIA meetings are great for local investors who want

to network and learn more about the topic. These meetings are usually beginner-friendly and are a great way for someone new to meet the local players. They can also help you find deals too.

One member of my 7 Figure Altitude program is currently netting $200K a year just from attending REIA meetings and buying flips from wholesalers in that group!

- **Networking Clubs**

    Sheri networks through Business Network International (BNI), a worldwide networking platform for various professionals such as attorneys, marketing agencies, real estate agents, investors, financial advisers, and contractors. BNI has an annual membership fee and time requirements, but it's well worth the effort. Sheri gets a handful of deals a year through her membership. There is a lot of money to be made in these groups, but someone with at least a few deals' worth of experience might find more traction than an amateur.

- **Agents**

    There are times when a real estate agent doesn't want to take on a property. Maybe the home won't sell for a high enough price to make the commission worth the effort. Perhaps the client is difficult to work with. Sometimes the agent is willing to take a smaller commission in exchange for working with someone who has cash in hand. Whatever the circumstances, real estate agents will gladly refer you to sellers they aren't interested in working with.

    Introduce yourself to local agents and explain the types of properties you're looking for. Let them know that you pay with cash and can close quickly.

    Flippers like the fact that agents can offer them

something wholesalers can't—a double commission. Here's how it works. The flipper and agent agree that if the agent sends the flipper a lead they close on, the flipper will then sell the house through the agent once it has been renovated. This means that the agent will earn a commission from the property twice: once when they buy and once when they sell.

If you're a house flipper, this type of arrangement is a no-brainer. Network with as many agents as possible!

- **Online Investing Groups**

    There are tons of online resources for real estate networking. Facebook groups, online forums, social media pages—the opportunities are endless. Jump into a community like my Facebook group to look for other investors in your area. You can meet new flippers and wholesalers to strategize and learn the business with, as well as seasoned investors who can help you navigate the path ahead (because they've been there).

- **Creative Strategies**

    When someone needs to sell their home, a real estate agent or wholesaler likely isn't the first person they'll talk to. Consider who else a motivated seller might want to discuss options with and introduce yourself to them.

    One brilliant way Sheri gets referrals is through senior care facilities. When an elderly person needs to move to assisted living, they often need to sell their home quickly. You can meet these folks by giving your information to local assisted-living facilities and in-home care providers.

    Other professionals a distressed seller might meet with include reverse-mortgage lenders, hospice care workers, estate planners, probate attorneys, and defense attorneys.

    As with most things in business, networking only works

if you can offer something of value in return. For example, probate attorneys—lawyers who work with the executors and beneficiaries of an estate—often work closely with the families of the deceased, who might want to sell the home quickly.

However, you shouldn't just walk into their office and ask, "Hey, probate attorney, can I have some leads please?" Instead, explain what you do and how it can add value for them and their clients.

And let's get this hard truth out of the way—when you're networking, the people you meet aren't going to care about the success of your business as much as you will. What they care about is their *own* business. So consider these options.

o   How can you help them achieve their goals?

o   Can you relieve a realtor of a stressed-out client or a condemned property?

o   Can you help a probate attorney quickly resolve an estate dispute or give them more business yourself on deals you come across first?

o   Maybe you can help a seasoned wholesaler branch out into a new zip code.

o   You could offer a wholesaler cash on hand in exchange for first choice of their deals.

Create mutually beneficial, long-lasting relationships that will help build your business and your reputation, and the deals will come to you.

Where Should You Start?

What's the best way to get deals? The answer depends on you.

I've mentioned a lot of different marketing strategies in this chapter. To figure out where to start, look at your strengths, your interests, and your personality.

- Do you have more time or more money?
- Do you have the capital to spend $2,500 per deal as well as the infrastructure to handle hundreds of calls per week?
- Or do you have the capital to invest in pay-per-click but can only handle a handful of inquiries per month?
- Are you great at running Facebook Ads? Ringless voicemail might work well if you have a full-time job elsewhere and can only respond during the evenings and weekends.
- Or are you a social butterfly who can network your way into great deals for free?

As you develop your marketing plan, keep the three warnings below in mind.

Warning #1: Don't assume it will work overnight.

You can't send out 50 mailers and expect a bunch of interested sellers immediately. Be patient. Give your chosen method enough time to actually produce results.

When I started, it took *four and a half months* to get just one deal. With direct mail, we've found that homeowners need to see six or seven mailers from us before they respond.

The last thing you want to do is quit halfway through your campaign. Chances are, the results you're seeking are right around the corner and you are inches from gold. Just keep going.

Warning #2: Do not try every strategy in this chapter at once.

Pick one or two and dedicate yourself to them. When I started wholesaling, I committed myself to direct mail for the first year, and that is why my company grew so quickly. Instead of attempting a dozen different strategies and hoping one sticks, become an expert at a single technique.

Once you choose a strategy, track and analyze the numbers, twist the dials, tweak your method, get good at it, ramp it up, then consider adding additional methods.

Warning #3: Don't pick a marketing strategy that you hate just because you think it will lead to the best results.

If you truly aren't comfortable cold-calling sellers, don't do it. If you're not awfully tech-savvy, don't choose internet marketing. If the strategy you think you "should" do isn't a good fit for your strengths or your personality, you're not going to be able to give it your all. And you need to be able to dive in headfirst with no reservations if you want to succeed.

Real estate investing takes grit and hustle and hard work, and you'll have to push yourself past your comfort zone no matter which strategy you choose. But don't set yourself up for failure by giving yourself a job you hate.

> **FLIGHT PLAN HANDBOOK:**
> **Choose A Marketing Strategy**
>
> Out of the strategies above, choose a marketing method to pursue. The best strategy for you is something that…
>
> - You can do consistently for several months in a row.
> - Fits within your budget.
> - Aligns with your strengths and interests.
>
> Find a handy SWOT analysis resource that is usually reserved for my 7 Figure Flipping clients in your Flight Plan Handbook at 7FFHandbook.com.

Now that you know how to reach sellers, you'll need to ready yourself for when the calls come in.

Chapter 10
Lead Intake Secrets

This is a short chapter because lead intake is a short—yet critical—job. It's imperative you know what to do and say when a lead calls you. I define a **lead** as anyone who contacts my company about a house they are interested in selling.

People who call and say, "I don't own that house anymore" or "Take me off your list" aren't leads. A true lead is someone who owns a piece of real estate and is interested in hearing what you have to say.

The Three Goals Of Lead Intake

You might be surprised to learn that at this stage, you won't be negotiating. You won't talk about how much you're willing to pay for the house or whether you'll take the deal. In fact, you won't discuss numbers at all. That comes much, much later.

At this stage, you have three responsibilities.

- **Gather Information:** Find out the key details behind why the person is contacting you. Do they have a house to sell? Where is the house? Why do they want to sell? You don't need to find out every possible detail, just the essentials.
- **Qualify The Lead:** Is the seller motivated? If so, how motivated? Are they ready to sell now, or should you reach out to them again in a few months? How much money do they want for the house?

- **Set The Appointment:** Schedule an in-person or phone appointment to meet with the seller at the property or to talk in more detail.

What To Do When A Seller Calls You

The phone rings. You answer. "Yes, hi—I saw your mailer and I want to know what you can offer me for the house."

Great! Your marketing worked.

At this moment, if you're new to the direct-to-seller marketing world, you might be feeling a little nervous or even panicky. You've got a lead on the phone, but what should you say?

On my first seller call, I freaked out. I was so nervous I didn't even want to answer the phone! But consider this—they are probably just as anxious as you. If you can solve their problem, that's all that matters.

Here's a checklist you can reference to get prepared for that first call.

- **Build rapport.**

    Get to know the seller. Ask them to tell you about the property, and look for opportunities to make a personal connection with them. "Oh, you have three little boys at home? We have three boys too!" Things like that. Try to find common ground and build some unforced rapport early in the call.

- **Answer questions.**

    The person calling probably doesn't understand the real estate ecosystem like you do. They may assume that selling their house means getting an agent involved, making repairs, and letting buyers walk through the place day after day. They might not understand where you come in or what you can offer. Don't worry about getting them to absorb your entire business model. Just explain that you buy properties as-is (no renovations needed) for cash and that you can close quickly.

- **Ease the caller's concerns.**

    Some callers will be angry. Others will be upset. Many will be overwhelmed. In response, empathize. Answer their questions. Be patient. And more than anything else, stay calm.

- **Gauge motivation.**

    Some people will be desperate for a quick transaction while others are just shopping around. Not everyone is ready to sell right away. Your job is to find the people who need help now and are truly motivated. Do they sound upset? Is the property in need of repairs? Listen for signs of distress.

- **Discover why the caller chose you.**

    A seller has many ways to sell a property, including listing it themselves and working with a real estate agent. So it's helpful to ask why they're calling you. Do they need cash immediately? Do they have an issue with their tenant? Did they inherit a property they don't want? This information will be critical when negotiations begin.

- **Learn their asking price (if possible).**

    While you don't want to reveal your target number or begin negotiations yet, you should try to find out approximately how much they want to sell for. This will give you a helpful benchmark when you begin negotiations later.

- **Set an appointment.**

    The biggest objective of this first call, and the goal of the entire lead intake process, is to schedule an appointment. You can either meet with the seller at the property or set up a phone call where your acquisitions rep can negotiate with them.

You might be saying, "Hang on…why would I schedule the appointment now if I haven't even determined whether the house is a good deal or not? Shouldn't I analyze it first?"

No. You should *always* set the appointment while you still have the seller on the phone. This is critical.

As soon as you hang up, your chances of ever hearing from them again drop by 50%. So if you've gathered a bunch of great info but then you tell the seller you'll run some numbers and call them back later, there's a very real chance you'll never actually reconnect with that person again.

> ### Pro Tip: How To Uncover An Asking Price
>
> A great lead intake manager has a few subtle ways of learning their asking price.
>
> Generally, they will start by asking the seller what amount they need to get for the house by saying something like…
>
>> If we can pay cash, close on a date of your choice, and you don't have to make any repairs or do anything to the house, what do you think you would get for the house?
>
> When asked, sometimes callers will simply give a number. But more often, they will typically respond, "You're the investor. You tell *me* what it's worth!"
>
> A savvy negotiator might try to learn the price of other houses in a similar condition.
>
> "I'm sure you have seen some other houses listed in the neighborhood lately. Do you have any idea what houses like yours sell for?"
>
> Or "If I had a magic wand and could give you exactly what you want, what would it be?"
>
> It might surprise you to learn that my team usually asks them what they want for the house at least seven times. If a caller still won't give a number, try using some humor. Throw out a crazy low or high number to try to get them to respond.
>
> "Well, if you don't know what the house is worth or what you want for it, would you take a hundred dollars? No? How about a million?"
>
> Sometimes rattling a caller is the only way to get them to open up. If your caller seems like the type who isn't easily offended, try: "If you don't know what you want to get for the house, how do you plan to sell it?" But in this case, be ready for an argument!

Once you've set the next appointment, it's time to analyze the deal.

Chapter 11
Master Deal Analysis

A few years ago, I lost $70,000 because of some train tracks.

I found a house near the coast of Florida that I wanted to flip. It was a high-end home, bigger and more complicated than any other project I had taken on by that point. I was still new to investing, but I had made good money on my recent flips, and as much as I hate to admit it, I might have been getting a little full of myself. A little cocky. A little too confident.

I funded the purchase of the property through the seller and renovations through a private lender. I had no personal money in this deal at all.

The house took a while to renovate, and the costs stacked up. But I knew it would be worth a lot when it was finished. This house was so nice, it had been featured on an episode of *Beach Hunters* on HGTV. I wasn't worried.

We wrapped up the repairs. I listed the house for sale with a local real estate agent.

And then…crickets.

No offers. No showings. Barely a hint of interest.

That's weird, I thought. I knew the house was priced fairly for the area. There were a few high-end homes nearby, and some of them had sold recently. It shouldn't have been that hard to find a buyer.

After a couple weeks of silence, I had a knot in the pit of my stomach. *There's something wrong here*, I thought. *I missed something*. But what?

"It's the train tracks," my agent explained. "The tracks that run right next to the property. The buyers I spoke to this morning told me they didn't even want to see the house because of them."

I had known about the train tracks from the start. Houses that back up to them tend to be worth less than houses that don't. I had factored this in when running the numbers on the deal and knocked a little off my expected after repair value (ARV), the price I wanted to sell the property for once I renovated. But I hadn't thought it would be *this* big of a problem. Additionally, this train track was rarely ever used and only ran every few days or so.

"Are you sure that's the reason?" I asked. "Maybe we just need to get this in front of more buyers."

"Everyone's saying the same thing," my agent said. "This is the third buyer this week who didn't even want to see the house—they saw the tracks and said no."

Well, shoot—I had miscalculated. But even then, I didn't know just how badly I had done so.

"Okay, go ahead and drop the price a little," I said.

We lowered the price. A week later, we lowered it again. Then again. And again.

By the time it sold, I had lost $70,000 on the deal.

Luckily, I had made enough money on my previous flips to pay my lender in full with interest—something you should *always* do, even if you personally have to swallow a loss.

But I learned a few hard lessons from that flip.

First, stay away from high-end houses in a market that doesn't have a lot of high-end houses. (Remember that list of flipping mistakes?) Buyers are much more selective when buying at the high end of any market, and something that would only reduce the value a little on a standard property, like nearby train tracks, can completely tank a high-end home.

But the most valuable thing I learned?

You *have* to get the numbers right before you buy. You must analyze every tiny detail of the deal accurately.

My ARV was way off because I didn't know how much the train tracks would bring down the value. I knew they *would* impact it, but I didn't build in a big enough discount when buying the house to account for that drop.

Since then, my team and I have completed hundreds of real estate deals, and we've only lost money on a couple of them.

I definitely don't want you to lose $70K (or more), so I'll show you how we analyze deals today to lock in our profit *before* we sign the contract.

It's All About The Offer Price

Repeat after me:

> If I buy the house at a discount, I *will* make money.

When it comes to analyzing a potential deal, your goal is to figure out what price you can offer the seller that will allow you to safely make a profit. All the other factors—what the house will be worth once it's repaired, cost to repair it, closing costs, and interest payments—are just part of getting to your maximum allowable offer (MAO).

The MAO is what matters. The only way to lose money on a deal is to buy it too high.

Yes, sometimes crazy unexpected issues that would have been impossible to foresee can arise during a project—like the real estate market could crash overnight or something—but occurrences like this are rare.

If you can get the MAO correct, you really don't need to worry too much about losing money on your deals. And that's a very comforting thought.

Is Deal Analysis Different For House Flippers And Wholesalers?

You might be wondering whether this process is different depending on whether you are a flipper or a wholesaler. Yes and no.

If you're a wholesaler, you'll need to leave room for your profit *and* your buyer's profit when analyzing the deal.

If you're a flipper, you'll only need to leave room for your own profit.

Other than that, the process is virtually the same.

For the purposes of this book, I'm going to walk you through how to analyze a deal from a house flipper's perspective. If you're a wholesaler, simply subtract your desired profit ($5,000 to $50,000 or whatever amount you want to build in) from the final MAO.

Make sense? Let's dive in!

Gathering Information

First, check that the seller's name matches the one on the deed. It's worth your time to ensure that the person you meet with is actually the owner of the house (and not a partner or family member). You need to speak with the person who can make the decision to sell.

Then, review the property's prior sales price and tax history in the county records. You want to know what the current owners paid for the property and how much it may have appreciated since then.

Take the time to double-check basic factors like these:

- Age of the home
- Amenities
- Lot size
- Neighborhood
- Number of rooms and bathrooms
- Square footage

All these factors will influence the ARV.

If you use free online data sites like Zillow, Trulia, or Redfin to evaluate the property, cross-reference county records for the square footage, which is often exaggerated or incorrect on these sites. Because you'll make some crucial decisions based on this information, use the official records on file with the county or city appraiser's office.

Once you're confident you have all the correct info, it's time to comp the property.

Comping Properties

Before you calculate your MAO and meet with a seller, you'll need to determine the house's ARV. If you're a wholesaler, it's what your buyer will sell it for. Think of this as the final price of the property.

The ARV is one of the first and most critical numbers you need to know. Everything else, including your MAO, depends on it.

To accurately determine the ARV of the property, you'll look at comparable sales, also known as comps.

A **comp** is simply another house similar to the one you're considering flipping that has recently sold in the same general area where your property is located. Comps are used to determine the going rate for houses in that area and are a good indication of what yours will ultimately sell for.

You can also look at homes that are currently listed on the market or under contract in your target area, but these aren't as strong as comps that have actually sold, and should only be used in the absence of that data.

To access data for comparable properties, you can use free online websites like Zillow. But to really get the most detailed information, you'll want to use the **Multiple Listing Service (MLS)**, which provides full details on properties that are either up for sale or have been sold on the open market.

To get access to the MLS, you'll likely need to work with a real estate agent or someone else in the industry, or you could become an agent yourself. Honestly, it's much easier to get MLS access than you might think. We have it in multiple states. For example, you can become an assistant to a real estate agent in many different markets and get your own MLS login.

> If the MLS isn't an option for you, you can find a cheap but powerful alternative to running comps in the Flight Plan Handbook.

Once you have your data, here's how to comp a property to determine the ARV.

Look at properties that have recently sold in your target area. They should contain the full range of features expected in a home like the one you're evaluating. They also should be in great shape, with no damage or blemishes. These are standard retail homes that any buyer in your target area would love. Pay close attention to how much these homes sold for, because your flipped house will be on par with these when you're finished with it.

Features That Impact Valuation

Higher	Lower
Two-car garage	Carport
Pool	Small yard
Walk-in master shower	Tub/shower combo
Stainless steel appliances	White or black appliances
Tiled kitchen floors	Laminated kitchen floors
New cabinets	Old cabinets

Next, look for some "as-is" comps. As the name implies, these are houses sold recently without any updates, or "as-is." They may or may not be as distressed as the property you're going to flip, but they clearly need some updating. You won't give these as much weight, but they give you an idea of the current value of your target property.

When reviewing these properties for comps, here are some specs to look for.

- Sold within the past 90 days
- Within a half mile of your target property
- Similar in size, square footage, bed/bath count, and age to your target property
- In the same or similar neighborhood

Finding comps is not an exact science. For example, if there are no properties similar to yours that have sold within the last 90 days, you can expand that to 180 days. Alternatively, you may want to stay within the last 90 days but increase the radius. The goal is to get a good picture of what your house is likely to sell for by comparing it to similar properties in a similar condition and in similar areas.

After looking at recently sold comps, you can expand your search to ones that are listed (up for sale) or pending (under contract with a buyer but have yet to close).

Currently listed properties help you understand the going rate in your market. If you see recently rehabbed houses that are not selling, take note of the price. You might not want to value your own property any higher.

Pending properties can project future values, but keep in mind that these might not sell for the price stated on the MLS. And unless you know the agent, you likely won't find out until the homes actually sell.

I would give little or no consideration to listed or pending short sales, which are houses being sold for less than the owners owe to their lenders. This is just a number an agent threw out to get an offer on a property. Often the bank hasn't done an appraisal or even an analysis of the property yet, so there is a good chance the short sale lender will never approve the sale at the listed price.

Your primary focus should be on properties that are similar after repairs to yours. But it's good practice to also pay attention to houses that are in the same as-is condition. If there are several comparable properties that have recently sold for (or are listed for) less than what you plan to offer, you could be overpaying.

Avoid using comps from a different city or school district, or across a major barrier such as a freeway, river, or railroad tracks. Also take into consideration swimming pools, garage size, lot size, views, and other upgrades so you can adjust your value accordingly.

Watch out for any unusual features in and around the home as well. Unsightly power lines, a driveway on a busy street, lack of parking, or a strange interior layout could all impact your ARV.

If the subject house only has one small bathroom for 2,000 square feet, be extremely careful. This is true even if the characteristic is atypical for the neighborhood. If you plan to invest in the only house with a steep driveway, no garage, or no patio, proceed with caution—without similar comps, you don't know how much these features might impact the ARV.

Finally, consider seasonal price changes for indications on both the resale value of your property as well as the best time of year to buy or sell. In most markets, properties sell higher during the summer. In very cold areas, the winter season could bring so much snow and bad weather that houses sit on the market until spring. Of course, this is all market dependent. A ski town, for example, might have higher prices during peak ski season.

Once you've found several comps that closely match your future finished product, you should have a pretty good idea of your ARV.

Here's an example that shows a typical process of using comps to find an accurate selling price.

Example: You find three flipped comps that have sold within the past two months and have the exact same floor plan as your subject property. To find recent flips, you examined the listing photos and the description. Everything was recently updated, so you think it might be a flip. Additionally, you found in the county records that the seller only owned the house a few months. What's more, the seller is listed as an LLC.

Let's say they sold for $160,000, $155,000, and $150,000. The home with the lowest sale price had laminate instead of granite countertops, which explains some variation in price. Because the other two had granite, so should yours after rehab.

You also notice one rehabbed property that has only been listed for five days. It was pending at $160,000 after just one day on the market. Additionally, you see another renovated property that has only been listed for two days and is priced at $165,000. This listing is still active.

Expected ARV: You can feel pretty confident that the ARV should be between $155,000 and $157,500.

Here's why: Your price isn't likely to go lower than $155,000 since another flipped property sold for that amount. Two houses have been listed higher than that recently, and one was pending quickly. That means $155,000 is a safe floor for your ARV.

You also know that one house is pending at $160,000 after just one day. This indicates it's likely that house is under contract close to the list price, since it was on the market for such a short time. It's reasonable to think that could happen with your investment property too.

Remember, the other two higher-priced listings haven't sold yet, and a lot can happen between contract and closing. That doesn't mean you can't safely push your ARV up a to the $157,500 range, but I wouldn't go higher in this case. That is, unless the situation changes. If the higher-priced houses close for $160,000 during your renovations, then great—you can increase your ARV.

Adjusting For Hidden Costs

Now that you've got your ARV, it's time to subtract the hidden costs.

There are four common hidden costs you need to be aware of when calculating your MAO.

- Financing Costs
- Holding Costs
- Purchase Closing Costs
- Selling Closing Costs

Financing Costs

If you're a flipper, chances are you'll borrow money to purchase the house and pay for repairs. (Soon I'll explain how to get funding for that.) For now, just know that various arrangements have varying fees, which you need to account for.

For example, if you borrow from a **private money lender**, or an organization or wealthy individual interested in providing a loan, expect to pay anywhere between 6% and 12% annualized return on your capital. If you use a **hard money lender,** you'll receive an asset-based loan secured by real property. In today's market, that might be around 12% annualized, with additional points and fees.

Most hard money lenders will charge you two to three **points**, or about 2% to 3% of the loan amount. Points are not annualized; you'll pay this on top of interest, regardless of how long you borrow the money.

If you pay a private lender or hard money lender 12% annualized, that's the same as 1% for each month you borrow the money. If it takes you four months to flip the property, you'll use that money for roughly the same amount of time. In this case, you need to calculate 4% of the total capital you'll borrow, and account for that when making your offer.

If you use hard money, also remember to calculate an additional 2% to 3% of the borrowed amount off the top. This comes out to between 6% and 7% for financing costs for a four-month period.

For example, if you borrow $100,000 from a money lender at 12% interest and two points, you pay 1% (or $1,000) a month for access to that money. If you hold the property for four months, you'd pay $4,000. In addition, you pay another 2% right out of the gate in points. In this example, your total fee to the money lender is $6,000 in financing costs to complete this project.

Holding Costs

Most new investors forget to take holding costs into consideration. **Holding costs** can include property taxes, home insurance, utilities, and maintenance (including lawn care, HOA fees, and snow removal.)

You need to know these costs because you'll pay them for as long as you own the property. If it takes you four months to flip and sell the house, you'll pay four months' worth of holding costs.

The best way to calculate how much this will cost is to ask the seller, or talk to another flipper or agent who works in the area. All this information should be readily available. If you can't get a good answer out of the seller for some reason, ask a couple of the neighbors what fees they pay.

Purchase Closing Costs

In every real estate transaction, the buyer and the seller each pay closing costs.

The **purchase closing costs** are the closing costs you incur when you first buy the house. When buying houses off the MLS, the seller pays the real estate agent commissions and many of the other closing costs. So when buying a property this way, your closing expenses will typically be less than when you sell the property later.

However, I've also taught you how to go directly to the seller for these properties. In that case, you pay all the closing costs on the front end for the seller (this is one reason they sell to us). But don't worry—since you do this without agents and go directly to the seller, the closing costs are typically close to those you'd have when you buy on the MLS.

I could spend a lot of time talking about purchase closing costs, but my goal is not to teach you about every single expense involved in buying a house. Instead, I just want to show you how to come up with your offer. So for now, just estimate that you will pay 2% of the purchase price at closing.

Selling Closing Costs

Closing costs can get a little expensive yet are often overlooked. As a reminder, **closing costs** include the fees paid when the purchase is finalized. If you work with an agent, you can expect to pay a commission of between 5% and 6% of the sale price.

Depending on the area and market, your buyer may ask for something called **concessions**, or a benefit offered to facilitate the deal. A common concession is agreeing to cover the closing costs. These can range anywhere from a few thousand dollars to 5% of the purchase price. Look for concessions in the

MLS when you are comping the property. They are usually near the financing details or special notes. You could also ask other agents if they are common in your area.

You will want to include at least 2% for additional closing costs, such as title, attorney fees, and escrow. However, this will vary significantly based on your area. If you are in New York, your attorney fees and taxes will be significantly higher than if you are selling a home in Alabama. So make sure to call a title company or attorney and get a sample Closing Disclosure (CD) or HUD-1 that has fees broken out for any house you are interested in. This will allow you to dial in this percentage before you even purchase the house to flip.

Overall, depending on the area and type of home you're dealing with, plan on paying anywhere from 8% to 10% of the sale price in closing costs. When calculating this to make your offer, assume the house will sell for its ARV.

Estimating Repairs

Holding costs depend greatly on how long you own the property. And *that* depends on your renovation timeline. So let's assess those repairs.

You can't effectively estimate how much repairs will cost solely based on the MLS or website. Without a physical or virtual walk-through, you'll miss something. As a result, you should arrive on-site prepared to do some mental math to get an accurate MAO. If you plan to work directly with the seller, you might need to calculate the MAO moments before sitting down to negotiate.

And yes, there *is* some guesswork involved in estimating repairs. But you can increase accuracy a few ways. For example, after signing the contract, you can hire a contractor to walk through with you to come up with an exact scope of work. For now, you just need a rough estimate so you can calculate your MAO.

Here's a quick checklist you can use to estimate repair costs as you walk through the property. In the beginning, you'll need to look up the cost of materials and labor, but eventually you'll get a good sense of pricing.

- **Appliances:** If you're flipping the house, you'll usually need to update old appliances. Does the refrigerator, oven, or dishwasher look outdated?

- **Bathrooms:** Bathroom renovations can be expensive. Does the house need new tile or an updated tub or shower? Many old houses need a complete bathroom remodel, but some can simply be refinished. Consider the price of a new vanity, lights, shower pan or tub, tile, mirrors, faucets, toilet, and flooring.

- **Exterior:** Note the condition of the siding, decks and porches, garage, and gutters. Does the siding need to be replaced or painted? The cost of labor will be much more for a home with Victorian wood siding versus vinyl or composite.

- **Interior:** Examine the drywall, fireplace, and flooring. You might need new doors, hardware, or baseboards.

- **Flooring:** Does the home need new hardwood, vinyl, tile, or carpeted floors? Flooring price is measured in square feet and varies based on materials needed. Hardwood floors can be refinished, but that could even cost more than replacing them with an engineered floor or vinyl tile.

- **Heating and Cooling:** Inspect the furnace, wall heaters, and air-conditioning units to determine whether they need to be replaced. One often overlooked item is duct work—if it's old or damaged, that could be a big expense.

- **Kitchen:** The kitchen is usually the focal point of a home. Expect to replace or upgrade cabinets, lighting, sink and faucet, garbage disposal, countertops, backsplashes, and flooring.

- **Electrical:** Replace old smoke detectors, light boxes, switches, outlet covers, light fixtures, ceiling fans, sconces, and exterior lights. Also consider the cost to rewire any additional demolition areas and to update electrical wiring.

- **Plumbing:** You might have to replumb the house, fix leaks, install new toilets, or fix or replace the hot water heater.

- **Painting:** Include the cost to paint both the interior and exterior.

- **Roof:** How long has it been since the roof was replaced? Depending on factors like size, pitch (steepness), and quality of material (metal or shingle), a new roof can be expensive.

- **Windows:** Are the windows single-pane or dual-pane? Are they aluminum, wood, or vinyl? Do they open easily? Flippers often update old windows with new ones or at the very least replace any panes that are cracked, broken, or fogged.

- **Landscaping:** Is the yard full of knee-high grass and fallen trees? Landscaping can be an overlooked expense.

Check out the lawn and trees to see if any debris needs to be removed or if the lawn must be mowed. If so, decide whether you'll handle it yourself or hire a landscaper.

- **Miscellaneous:** Consider extra expenses like new locks and hardware, home inspections, pest control, demolition costs, and cleaning fees.

Some choices will be easy to make. Broken window? That needs to be fixed. But sometimes it won't be so clear. For example, it's on trend to install new stainless steel appliances in every full renovation. That may change in the future, and some lower-end houses may get black or white appliances instead of stainless steel. Also, some flippers don't replace fridges on their projects even if they replace the other appliances.

Here's my take: Look at the other houses that are selling in that neighborhood and update your investment to match. As a general rule, kitchens and bathrooms sell houses, and paint does a lot to make things look new and clean.

Don't forget to include a contingency for unanticipated or hidden costs. On your initial walk-through, you likely won't crawl into the attic or under the home to check for cracks, moisture, or issues with structural support (but a home inspector might). The older the home, the larger your buffer should be.

Estimating the cost of repairs isn't easy, especially if you are unfamiliar with remodeling. It will take time and experience to get good at this. Don't be afraid to ask other house flippers for feedback on the accuracy of your estimates.

If you're a wholesaler, do your best to estimate repair costs accurately—*but don't freak out or overthink it.* At the end of the day, you don't know which specific issues your buyer will want to remedy, and you can't possibly know the exact amount they will pay for the renovations they decide to make.

Some flippers are contractors themselves, while others have to hire out the work. Others might only make minor changes, while some might decide to gut the property. If your buyer is a landlord, they might put a lot of money into renovations, or they might rent it out as-is. You just don't know.

If you're a wholesaler, don't get caught up in estimating it exactly right every time. I struggled with this when I first started. I wanted to dial in the renovation budget as if I would be flipping it myself.

Try to get your repairs as close as possible, but don't let this stop you from making an offer. Jump in, get the contract signed, and then see what response you get from your buyers. If no one bites on the deal, your MAO is probably too high, and you will know better for next time. If multiple buyers get into a bidding war, your MAO is probably lower than it should have been.

Calculate Your Maximum Allowable Offer

By now you've comped the property and determined the ARV. You've calculated your purchasing, holding, financing, and closing costs. You've also estimated your repair costs.

Now it's time to calculate your MAO.

To do this, simply deduct your profit from the total.

If you're a flipper, solve this equation:

ARV - Purchasing/Holding/Closing/Financing Costs - Estimated Repairs - Profit = MAO

If you're a wholesaler, remember you'll need to include your profit. Solve this equation:

ARV - Purchasing/Holding/Closing/Financing Costs - Estimated Repairs - Buyer's Profit - Your Profit = MAO

How much profit should you include for the buyer? That's up to you, but in general, most flippers want to make $20K for the first $100K of the ARV, then an additional $10K for every $100K after that.

So if the ARV of the house is $300,000, a flipper would probably look for $40,000 in profit.

A Simpler Formula

You've learned a lot in this chapter, and it might seem confusing or difficult to calculate all of this for every house you look at. So here's a quick word of advice:

Don't let all these numbers stop you from making offers.

It's important that you understand the entire deal analysis process. That's why I took the time to explain it step-by-step. But trying to do all this math in your head while walking through a property with a seller might seem daunting.

Here's a simpler formula that will get you close enough to make solid offers. Just multiply your ARV by 0.85 and subtract profit and repair costs. This assumes that the purchasing, holding, finance, and closing costs are 15% of the ARV. As I said in the previous sections, this will vary depending on the flipper and location.

How do you drive that number down? Get cheaper money (meaning better terms), negotiate a lower listing rate with your agent, and reduce the hold times by getting more efficient so you can flip faster.

For Flippers: (ARV x 0.85) - Estimated Repairs - Your Profit = MAO

For Wholesalers: (ARV x 0.85) - Estimated Repairs - Buyer's Profit - Your Profit = MAO

> For example, let's say I find a potential investment property. I look up comps for similar renovated houses in the area. Using these similar properties, I estimate the ARV at $200,000. To account for holding, closing, and financing costs, I multiply by 0.85.
>
> **$200,000 x 0.85 = $170,000**
>
> The property needs an estimated $25,000 in repairs, so I subtract that cost from my MAO.
>
> **$170,000 - $25,000 = $145,000**
>
> I plan to wholesale this house. I estimate that an investor buyer would want to make around $30,000 profit on the deal.
>
> **$145,000 - $30,000 = $115,000**
>
> Now I know I can probably sell the contract for $115,000. I want to make $15,000 as my wholesale fee.
>
> **$115,000 - $15,000 = $100,000**
>
> My MAO as a wholesaler is $100,000. But if I flipped this property, I could raise that to $115,000.
>
> Of course, when I meet with the seller, I'm not going to start negotiating at $100,000. I would probably start around $70,000 and work my way up.
>
> Keep that in mind. Your MAO shouldn't be the first offer amount you present. You'll need to leave yourself room to negotiate.

The bottom line is, do your due diligence—but don't let it stop you from making offers!

> **FLIGHT PLAN HANDBOOK:**
> **Practice Calculating MAO**
>
> Accurate MAOs make a deal less risky. Therefore it's in your best interest to get comfortable with this simple calculation. Let's practice.
>
> 1. Look for a home for sale on a free site like Zillow.
> 2. Calculate the ARV, as-is value, and cost to repair based on the photos available.
> 3. What's your MAO?
>
> The next time another wholesaler sends you a wholesale property, do the analysis yourself and see where you land on the numbers.

With your MAO ready, it's time to attend that meeting you set up with the seller. Yes, it's time to start negotiating!

Chapter 12
Expert Acquisitions

Donna lived in a modest house 40 minutes outside Nashville, not far from the Cumberland River. She had lived there most of her life, and now in her eighties, she shared the space with her grandson and great-grandson.

One afternoon in July of 2019, after getting one of our postcards, Donna called Blackjack Real Estate. It was a call that Val, my lead intake manager, would never forget.

Old age had taken most of Donna's hearing, and with it, much of her ability to speak. She had a hard time making herself understood and an even harder time understanding others.

But what she told Val on the phone was unmistakable.

"My grandson is stealing my Social Security checks. He's taking them to the bank and putting them in his own account."

"That's awful!" Val said. "Did you call the police?"

"My grandson says it's legal. He says I signed something. I just want to get away from him."

"He lives with you?"

"Yes," Donna said. "But it's my house. I own it. I want to sell it and get away from him."

It was a horrible story. As Val dug deeper, she learned more. Donna's grandson Jacob was in his early twenties with a kid of his own. His girlfriend and their child also lived there, and he claimed he was using Donna's Social Security checks to help pay the bills.

But Donna knew that wasn't true—she was paying all the bills herself from her own meager savings. Jacob wasn't helping out around the house either. The home was falling apart and needed major repairs.

It seemed like a textbook example of distress that a real estate investor could solve. We could step in, buy the house quickly with cash, and get Donna the money she needed to start over somewhere far away from her grandson. It *should* have been an easy deal.

There was just one problem.

Donna wanted $300,000 for the house.

Fully renovated, the house would have been worth maybe $275,000 at the most. And it definitely needed major work.

But Donna wouldn't budge on the price.

Most real estate investors would have backed off at this point. Talking to Donna was already difficult due to her hearing and speech impairments. The messy situation with her scheming grandson made things even worse. And with her asking for way more than the home was worth, it was tempting to politely end the conversation and move on to the next lead.

But when you understand how to build rapport, negotiate, and find win-win solutions, you can turn horrible deals into winners.

And that's why Val didn't hang up the phone that day.

Even though the deal seemed dead on arrival, Val knew that if she could get Donna to meet with Chad King, my acquisitions manager, everything would change. Chad could get to know her, understand her motivation, draw out the issues, and strategize a solution. If there was a deal to be done, Chad would make it happen.

This isn't something every real estate investor instinctively knows how to do. Knowing *what to say and how to say it* when meeting with sellers is what sets incredible negotiators like Chad apart.

Val scheduled an in-person appointment and passed the lead along to Chad. He ran the numbers, prepped for the meeting, and drove out to the house.

When he arrived, Donna told him, "I told her on the phone I want $300,000. I know what it's worth. You can sell it for more than that once it's fixed up."

Chad had seen all the comps from recent sales in the neighborhood and knew that after repairs it would barely go for what she wanted as-is. To make the deal work, we would have to get the house for around $170,000. But Chad didn't tell Donna that...at least not right away.

Instead, he simply smiled. "That's okay, ma'am. Let's see if we can figure something out. May I come in?"

For the next three hours, Chad sat with Donna and let her tell her story. He just listened.

She had no family nearby other than her grandson and his son. No car. No email address. She didn't even have a bank account in her name. Her only method of communication was an old flip phone her sister Beverly had given her. She had nowhere to go after selling the house—she just wanted out.

Her hearing was so bad that Chad had to write down some of his questions for her to read. And her speech was so bad that she had to write down some of her responses.

But as the story unfolded, and as Donna began to feel heard and respected and safe, everything changed.

Chad told her he couldn't buy the house until he knew she had somewhere to go. She mentioned possibly moving somewhere near her sister Beverly in Arkansas. Chad pulled out his phone and began looking at real estate listings there. He showed several to Donna.

Together, in that meeting and an additional four-hour meeting later that week, they put together a plan. Chad called a real estate agent in Arkansas where Beverly lived. He helped Donna find a house that she liked and hired a moving company. They ran the numbers on what it would cost for her to buy that small home and pay the moving expenses. They also priced out a small car, a new phone, and the money Donna would need to live the rest of her life comfortably. All this was done before a contract was signed or a price was established.

That number they came up with together became the contract price: $180,000. A little higher than we were aiming for, but Chad knew the deal would still work. After that first meeting with Chad and call with Val, Donna never mentioned the price $300,000 again.

We ended up wholesaling the house to a local flipper, who did a great job fixing it up. I believe he later sold it to a landlord, who rented it out. With Chad's help, we sold Donna's house and also purchased her new home simultaneously. He even helped her load the moving truck.

Sounds like a win-win and case closed, right? Don't forget about her grandson Jacob. On learning about the deal, his face turned red. Soon he was screaming at Donna. Chad had to physically step between them to defuse the situation.

This story is a great example of the real estate ecosystem in action. But it's an even better example of the *art of acquisitions*.

Chad didn't argue with Donna about what her house was worth. He didn't explain our business model and how we had to be at a certain number for it to work. He didn't pull out comps or try to convince her of the cost of the repairs needed. He didn't try to *talk* Donna into accepting his offer. Instead, he *listened*. He got to know her. And he helped her solve her problem in a mutually beneficial way.

A couple months later, Chad called Donna to check in on her. She was living comfortably a few blocks from her sister in Arkansas. She had a car and a bank account and was keeping every penny of her Social Security checks.

She said, "What you did was the nicest thing anyone's done for me."

We only made $5,000 profit on that deal. Like I said, we bought it a little higher than we had planned to. But getting to keep $5,000 after helping an elderly woman out of a bad situation…that's worth way more in my book. And I know Chad, Val, and the rest of the team at Blackjack Real Estate would agree.

How many investors do you think would have done all this for Donna? Especially considering she initially wanted more than the ARV? Where in that whole process would most people have quit on her? The initial call, the first appointment, the new house purchase, the moving truck, or when Jacob started yelling at her? Most investors would have taken the easy route. But that's what separates the elite from the ordinary.

Smart investors understand the power of building rapport and creative problem-solving. And they want to support their sellers.

When you understand the negotiation process, you can make money from nightmare deals like this one, without ever fighting over the price.

Direct-To-Seller Acquisitions

When Chad goes on a seller appointment, he knows that he will deal with a distressed property. He anticipates damage such as sunken foundations and collapsed roofs. He's good at estimating the repair costs and MAOs. He knows how much it costs to rehab a bathroom or renovate a kitchen. He knows the ARV and how much he can sell the property for to another investor.

But these aren't the only reasons he is remarkable at his job.

Chad is skilled at uncovering and solving problems for the seller.

If someone is considering giving up equity in exchange for a fast and hassle-free sale, that means something is going on.

What is their motivation for selling the house?

Why does it need to happen fast?

How can we add value or solve a problem that no one else can?

When you're buying a house directly from the seller, you are the real estate expert. No agents will be involved. That means it's up to you to steer the deal.

The seller may not know much about real estate. If they have lived in the house for decades, it may have been a long time since they have been part of a real estate transaction. You may need to educate them on the basics. You'll need to act as their guide, talking them through the language of the contract. You might have to teach them about earnest money, due diligence, inspection periods, and closing dates.

Remember, not only are they financially tied to the property, they may also be emotionally invested. Maybe they're selling their childhood home or an inheritance from a deceased family member. Maybe they planted trees in the backyard that are now 30 years old.

All of these factors and more could be involved in the sale. Despite the seller's financial and emotional ties to the property, you have to help them realize that selling their home below market value is a win-win option.

If it's *not* a win-win option, you shouldn't be meeting with them at all. To get a house at a discount, there *has* to be distress—some kind of motivation, a problem you can help them solve. Remember, they are trading equity for the service you provide, and it takes a particular set of circumstances for the transaction to be mutually beneficial.

If you're a house flipper, your MAO can be higher, giving you a little more room during negotiations. But wholesalers, you'll need to invest a lot of time and money to find motivated sellers and learn to problem-solve and negotiate well, because you need to buy houses for less than other investors do.

Seller Meeting And Negotiation Steps

Your goal, when arriving at a seller's house for an appointment, should be to *get the contract signed that same day*. If you go into the meeting expecting that it will probably take a few tries to get the contract signed, you're not going to appear confident and competent.

Start by getting your mindset right. Know that you can help the seller. Plan to get the contract signed. Expect that you'll get the deal. And walk in like you have a million dollars in your pocket!

Below is the 11-step process Chad follows when going on appointments.

> **#1:** Call to confirm the appointment.
> **#2:** Greet the seller and set the frame.
> **#3:** Tour the property.
> **#4:** Build rapport and gain critical knowledge.
> **#5:** Identify smoke screens and potential objections.
> **#6:** Discuss the situation and find motivation.
> **#7:** Talk numbers and drop a price anchor.
> **#8:** Negotiate the deal.
> **#9:** Sign the contract.
> **#10:** Set expectations for what will happen next.
> **#11:** Send the contract to your title company.

Let's take a closer look at how this is done.

#1: Call to confirm the appointment.

If the appointment was set by a lead intake manager, like Val at my company, call the seller a few hours beforehand to confirm that they're still available.

New members of the 7 Figure Runway and 7 Figure Altitude mastermind groups often tell me they prefer not to confirm the appointment because they're worried the seller will cancel. While I understand that it's tough seeing a deal dissolve before you even get a chance to meet, I strongly recommend calling ahead.

If a seller decides they don't want to meet after all, that means they likely would have stood you up or declined your offer anyway. And if you *don't* confirm, they might forget about the appointment. The check-in call gives you an opportunity to continue building rapport and, if they do want to cancel, it gives you the opportunity to re-sell them on why they should still meet with you.

When you go to the meeting, you'll need to bring a few things. Get a clipboard and use it to carry your documents in one place.

Here's what Chad brings to appointments.

- Blank purchase contract
- Amounts the property was previously bought and sold for
- Any appraisals
- Comps, ARV, as-is value, and MAO
- Cost-to-repair checklist
- County tax records showing ownership of the house
- Square footage, year built, bedrooms, bathrooms, and acreage

Bring these documents and details with you, but don't dump them all on the seller right away. Instead reference them as needed, and *only* as needed, during the negotiation process.

#2: Greet the seller and set the frame.

After meeting the seller, immediately set the frame for the appointment. This is one of Chad's top recommendations that helps him close more deals. There's a lot of tension in the air before negotiations. Creating a clear road map free of surprises is one way to ease the process.

What does it mean to set the frame? Simple—you tell the seller what's going to happen at the appointment.

For example, Chad will say something like...

> Thanks very much for inviting me over. Would you mind if I took just one minute to share how these appointments usually go?
>
> First, I'd love for you to give me a tour of the property. I'll snap a few photos while we walk and get to know each other a bit. After the walk-through, I'd like to sit down with you to better understand your situation and what benefit we can bring you.
>
> I will be able to put together an offer for you today. If you love it, great—we are prepared to purchase the property on-site. If for any reason it's not going to work for you, that's completely okay too. We certainly don't buy every house we look at.
>
> Is there anything else you were hoping to accomplish today?

You don't have to say all this verbatim, but it's crucial to tell the seller how the meeting will go so they aren't caught off guard by anything.

- Explain that you will take pictures, so they don't react when you pull out your phone.
- Let them know that you want to spend time learning more about their situation so they understand that you are there to help them.

- Assure them that you don't buy every house you look at, which suggests that you won't be pushy and that you aren't desperate for the sale.

- Most importantly, make sure they know you have a contract in hand if they are willing to sign. You do not want it to be a surprise when you pull out the agreement.

Pro Tip: Use the word "agreement" instead of "contract" during negotiations. I've found that contracts make homeowners feel like they need to proceed with caution or get an attorney involved. An agreement, on the other hand, is a bit less formal and gives the seller the confidence to review the terms on their own.

#3: Tour the property.

You should document everything—the good and the bad. Look for problems. Do your best to get an accurate representation of the home. If you're a wholesaler, you're going to show these pictures to investors later. They won't want to work with you if you try to hide issues.

If possible, do a video walk-through. A solid video can potentially help you sell the contract sight-unseen. Additionally, every photo of an issue with the house is an opportunity to ask the seller about it. Usually they will volunteer an explanation as you go to take a photo of a problem area.

This happens all the time. On one property walk-through, I saw a stain on the ceiling, so I stopped to snap a few pictures. Without so much as a word from me, the seller immediately told me a story about a leaky roof.

"What do you think it will take to fix it?" I asked.

"I'll probably need to replace the roof."

Bingo! Now I had useful information to help negotiate the price.

It's imperative that *the seller is with you during the tour.* That's because it's only partially about the house; it's also your best opportunity to build rapport with them. Some sellers will just open the front door and say, "Go ahead, walk through!" Don't do it. Ask the seller to walk with you and tell you about the house. Get them talking. Listen to what they say. Ask questions. This connection is crucial.

#4: Build rapport and gain critical knowledge.

You want to make the seller feel more comfortable by getting to know them. Build rapport by asking them what they do for a living, where their kids go to school, or where they intend to move.

Each question is a pathway to valuable information that will factor in to the negotiation. For example, their occupation might clue you in to their income level. The location of their new home could lead to a discussion about why they need to move in a hurry. Don't just get surface-level answers.

A seller once told me they were moving because they wanted to downsize. With a little more probing, I learned that the real reason was that she had a two-year-old granddaughter with medical issues and needed to move to North Carolina immediately so they could be closer to the care she needed. That's a lot more urgent than downsizing.

But what exactly can you say to get the seller comfortable enough to disclose this kind of information? Chad uses multiple sales strategies that he learned from other exceptionally successful sales coaches, trainers, and a lot of books.

Here are a few of the top methods: mirroring, labeling, and Socratic questioning.

Mirroring

Mirroring is the practice of repeating key words or the last few words that the seller says, combined with an upward inflection to pose it as a question. This encourages the seller to elaborate. From the book *Never Split the Difference*, author Chris Voss describes mirroring like this:

> Mirroring will make you feel awkward as heck when you first try it. That's the only hard part about it; the technique takes a little practice. Once you get the hang of it, though, it'll become a conversation Swiss Army knife, valuable in just about every professional and social setting.

For example, if the seller says something like, "The mortgage on this property is just too high," Chad might respond, "The mortgage is too high?" From there, he might learn that the seller hasn't been able to pay the mortgage for a few months or that they recently lost their job. He will likely also get them to tell him what the mortgage payment is.

Mirroring is an instinctual, intuitive way to connect with strangers. It makes the seller feel that you hear what they're saying, which helps them relate to you, puts them at ease, and encourages them to volunteer more information.

Labeling

Labeling is similar to mirroring, but instead of simply repeating what the seller says, you characterize and reframe their emotions or situation.

For example, if a seller says something like, "I don't have time to work with a real estate agent—I need the money by next week," Chad might label their situation by saying, "Yeah, it takes time for those deals to go through. It sounds like you're in a *tight* position." Or he might say, "Seems like you cannot wait for it to sit on the market."

Now the seller's situation has been labeled as tough or stressful, which not only shows them that you understand what they are going through, it also suggests that you can help solve their problem.

Socratic Questioning

Another method Chad uses is Socratic questioning, or the art of asking open-ended questions as a way to encourage conversation and discover answers. Examples of Socratic questions include the following:

- When you say _____, what do you mean?
- You must have brought that up for a reason. What is it?

In a real estate negotiation, these questions might sound like…

> Seller: "You know we are just looking to get a fair price."
>
> You: "Absolutely, I can appreciate that. When you say 'fair price,' what do you mean?"
>
> Seller: "We could certainly hold on to the place, but if your offer is reasonable, we'd sell."
>
> You: "Understood. When you say reasonable, what did you have in mind?"

These open-ended, judgement-free questions can quickly uncover any information you need to ensure the sale can go through. You'll be surprised by the kinds of things people will share when you employ this strategy.

One seller told Chad he was ready to get rid of his investment property because it was "too much of a hassle." Chad mirrored the seller by asking, "Oh, owning property can be a real hassle?"

"Yeah, we had to evict the last tenant," the seller elaborated, "because they stole the appliances and didn't pay rent for six months."

During later negotiations, Chad remembered the problems the seller had with the last tenants. He paired that information with labeling to help them reach an agreement on terms. "I know we're a little far apart on the price, but it seems like you're trapped by this property. Do you want to renovate it and watch another tenant destroy it?" By labeling the landlord as "trapped," he was able to get the property under contract for $5,000 below his MAO.

Mirroring, labeling, and Socratic questioning are fantastic tools. It's amazing what people will disclose when they see that you have a genuine interest in their lives and are willing to listen. Not only can these questions build rapport and draw out motivation, they can also help you uncover any deal-killers.

#5: Identify smoke screens and potential objections.

There are three big objections you need to watch out for.

- Closing timeline
- Competitors

- Hidden stakeholders

If you don't get these issues resolved during that first appointment, there's a good chance you'll lose the deal. As Chris Voss says, "The reasons why a counterpart will not make an agreement with you are often more powerful than why they will make a deal, so focus first on clearing the barriers to an agreement."

Closing Timeline

Find out the seller's time frame to close and whether they are ready to sign a contract that same day. If not, you're not in a position to negotiate a deal. If the seller wants to get out of the house in three months and needs time to make other living arrangements before they can sell, you need to know this early in the conversation. The last thing you want is to negotiate for two hours and *then* find out the homeowner isn't ready to sell yet.

These three smoke screens aren't the only problems you'll run into. A common objection we get is "I'm interested, but I need some time to think about it." In that situation, Chad will first try to get to the root of the hesitation by saying something like…

> I understand you need to think about it. I can certainly appreciate that. After 20 years in this house, all the memories you have in here, all the stress it's going to take to move, I can understand you wanting to think about it. Let me ask you a question though: What about doing business with me today has you concerned?

If the reason they want more time doesn't come to light, Chad may create urgency by showing the seller that our fast-cash offer may not be available for long. He might say something like...

> I know it's a lot to think about. I completely understand. But I have more houses to see today and this week. If I buy this one, I might not buy one of the others. And if I buy one of the others, I might not be able to buy this one. So unfortunately, we are going to have to call this a no. I just can't leave an open contract with you.
>
> But I want you to know it's okay. I don't expect to buy every house I see. Are you okay with me taking my offer off the table?

If the seller wants more time because other investors are looking at the property, you can use the following approach. In these cases, Chad might say something like...

> Listen, I can appreciate that you want to get the highest price, and I certainly will offer you as much as I possibly can. I'm simply not interested in getting into a bidding war with other people that I do not know. How am I supposed to know if the offers are apples to apples, or even if they are legitimate investors? If that is the route you want to go though, I do understand. No hard feelings here.

At that point, you must be willing to walk away from the deal if needed. You can also employ the carrot tactic and try to circle back at the end of the circus of investors. That sounds like this:

> I told you I'd be around $120,000 with our offer. I can certainly see if we have any wiggle room,

as well as whether we could put together a creative offer for you. With that being said, how about you go ahead and collect the other offers you planned on getting. Then I can sharpen my pencil and come back this afternoon after your last showing to give you my highest and best offer. Sound fair?

However you locate potential objections, do it gently. Don't just walk in and ask, "Are all the stakeholders here, are you ready to close today, and have you gotten other offers?" You'll likely get the door slammed in your face. Instead use mirroring, labeling, and Socratic questioning to slowly pull out the information you need. Otherwise you'll come across as abrupt, harsh, cold, or even needy.

A direct question like "Are all the stakeholders here?" should become a more subtle "If you sold the house today, is there anyone you'd need to call before making that decision?" The *way* you speak is just as important (if not more so) than *what* you say. With a small adjustment like this, the entire feel of the question changes and allows the sellers to open up.

Competitors

Don't assume you're the only real estate investor the homeowner has spoken with or will speak with. You'll definitely want to know if a seller is meeting with other investors or real estate agents up front rather than getting blindsided by a different offer later in the process.

Chad usually says something like, "I know we aren't your only option—we might not even be the best option for you. Have you spoken to a real estate agent about listing the property?"

If the answer is yes, that doesn't mean you can't negotiate a deal. Your MAO may not be as high as the agent's sale price, and it might be lower than some of the other offers the seller has received, but don't just give up immediately. You might be able to offer terms that entice the seller to trade more of their equity in return for your offer.

And don't underestimate the power of building real, authentic rapport. We've beaten higher offers many times because the seller decided we were honest and easy to work with compared to other investors.

Hidden Stakeholders

Don't assume that the homeowner is the only person who needs to agree to your terms even if they are the only name on the deed. And don't assume that the person who calls you about selling their home is the owner. Make sure all the stakeholders and decision influencers are present for the appointment and, during the meeting, find out if there's anyone else who needs to be involved.

- Does the homeowner have a spouse?
- Do they have children?
- What about a family member in real estate who may want to review your offer?
- Who else might object to the deal?
- Is there another person in the house whose opinion could influence it?

Get all this out of the way early in the negotiation. If there are hidden stakeholders, you will need to get them all on board before the deal will close.

#6: Discuss the situation and find motivation.

Before you start to talk numbers, revisit the reason the seller called you in the first place. Even if you've already discussed it, bring it up again. You must get the seller to start the negotiation in *the same emotional state* they were in when they made the decision to contact you.

When Chad sits down to negotiate, he usually starts by asking something like…

"What made you decide to give us a call?"

"What were you hoping I/we might be able to do for you?"

"How can we help?"

You can't offer them the full price for the property, so instead you should offer a solution to their problem. Ask yourself, "What can I offer them other than money that no one else can?" Sometimes it's a fast transaction or a cash purchase. Often it takes a little more creativity.

Remember how Chad helped Donna work out her next steps in life and find a new place to live? That effort on his part is why we won the deal. He was able to offer her something that most other investors or real estate agents wouldn't—he helped solve her *actual* problem, which wasn't the house. It was her abusive living situation, her loneliness, hopelessness, and dependence on others for survival.

But that's just one problem and solution. There are plenty of others that can tilt the deal in your favor and help you beat any competitors who may come knocking.

My company has done a lot of escrow holdbacks when sellers aren't able to move out of their properties immediately. This gives us assurance that they will move out by a certain date and allows us to complete the property sale while it's still occupied by the owner, giving them the flexibility to gather their belongings and make arrangements while the house is being sold.

For example, if we agree on a sale price of $100,000, we could give them $90,000 at closing and hold $10,000 until they move out on a predetermined date in the future. Then if they don't move out by that date or do damage to the property, they would forfeit the $10,000 holdback.

The seller won't always know what their options are. To figure out how he can improve the deal for a seller, Chad will ask, "Let's say we agree on price. Besides that, what else matters to you?"

We've gotten many deals by tailoring our offer to the seller's needs, even when our purchase price was lower than others the seller had already received. In one case, we got a house under contract for $15K less than a competitor because we allowed the seller's tenant to stay in the home for six months after closing.

These details matter. The first step of the negotiation is to figure out what problem you can solve.

#7: Talk numbers and drop a price anchor.

Always let the seller state their price first. You'd feel pretty sorry for yourself if you threw out your MAO and the seller would have sold for less. More importantly, you don't want to insult them. In all likelihood, they aren't going to like your number. If you surprise them with a low one, they might just ask you to leave. By getting them to give you a price first, you can better understand how much room you have to negotiate—and whether the deal is closeable at all.

Sometimes a seller will throw out a price lower than your MAO. When this happens, don't just immediately accept it. If you do, the seller will wonder why you accepted so quickly or whether they could have asked for more. Counter everything, even good deals.

But you don't always have to counter with a different price. If your MAO is $80,000 and the seller wants $70,000, you might say, "Fine, but I'm going to have to change the closing date from twenty-one days to forty-five." You may not have needed more time to close on the property, but it's imperative that the seller doesn't leave the table wondering if they could've gotten more. In an effective negotiation, the seller will feel like both parties are compromising.

How To Ask For A Price

Asking for a price can be hard. Here are a few of my team's go-to questions and responses to help open up negotiations.

- "How much do you need out of this place to get to [ideal outcome]?"
- "Have you thought about what you would need to get?"
- "Seems like you have a price in mind." (label)
- "You strike me as someone who's got their bottom-dollar number already penciled out."
- "After all is said and done, and the mortgage/liens are paid off, how much were you hoping to put in your pocket?"

Just because you got a price doesn't mean you are obligated to dive into the negotiation. If you haven't eliminated all the potential objections and smoke screens, keep moving forward with the process.

Another great way to ask for a price is to listen to the seller during the property tour. They may drop subtle statements implying that they have done some research. If that's the case, it's wise to use a Socratic question to get their figure.

Note: Just because you ask this question does not mean you are obligated to go into the negotiation. You can absolutely continue through the diagnosis at your own pace.

> You: "So when it comes to the property, what are you needing to make sense of selling the home?"
>
> Seller: "I don't know. We're just looking for a reasonable price."
>
> Me: "When you say 'reasonable price,' what did you have in mind?"
>
> Seller: "Well, we were really thinking between eighty and ninety thousand..."

If you don't want to make a joke, toss out a believable number that is lower than your MAO. For example, if your MAO is $65,000, say, "Did you know that some houses in this neighborhood are selling for $45,000?" This is called a **price anchor**. By stating this low price, the seller now has the number $45,000 anchored in their mind, which will make your higher MAO of $65,000 seem much more reasonable.

When you drop the price anchor, the seller might say something like, "I'd never sell for $45,000! I want at least $80,000" or "That seems low, but I'd consider $55,000." Now you're getting somewhere. Try these as well:

- "Some investors are buying them around here for [amount]. What do you think about that?"
- "Some houses around here have sold for as low as [amount]."

- "Take a look at these." (Hand seller a list of comps.)
  - "Are you familiar with these homes?"
  - "Where are they? How do they compare to yours? What did they sell for?"

Another way to get the dialogue started is to ask, "What do you think a company like ours would buy your house for?" or "Do you know what investors are paying for properties in this neighborhood?" Notice I'm not asking what renovated homes are selling for, because I don't want to reverse-anchor them high and have to get them down. My question is designed to talk about the lower-end comps.

I wish I had known what a price anchor was when I started negotiating with sellers. Instead, I'd go back and forth, trying to get the seller to give me a price. Three hours later (on a Saturday morning when I wanted to be eating breakfast and spending time with my family instead of sitting on this guy's couch), I'd find out the seller expected full retail value.

Sometimes the seller's reaction to your price anchor saves time by revealing that the deal isn't closeable.

#8: Negotiate the deal.

Once you start talking numbers, avoid giving anything without getting something in return. For example, if you ask for $55,000 and the seller says no, don't just say, "How about $60,000?" Instead, say something like, "If I was able to do $60,000, are you ready to get the agreement done today?" Don't immediately shoot up to your MAO. Your first offer should be far enough below the MAO that it's a little uncomfortable to make. You don't want to get thrown off their property, but you also want room for negotiation.

You can also discuss repairs as part of negotiating price. If you're $15,000 apart, ask them what they think it would cost to fix the foundation or replace the roof. Sellers often underestimate repair costs. Explain how much those repairs will *actually* cost, and subtract that amount from the price.

Before discussing the final offer, negotiate the terms of the close. For example, if Chad's MAO is $65,000, his most recent offer was $60K, and the seller's price is $70K, he might say something like...

> I don't have much more wiggle room here. I'm going to make a quick call to see if I can increase it by a few thousand. But if I can get $65,000 authorized by the owner, I need to know we can get the agreement done today.

Or try something like this:

> I don't think we can pay that much for the property. That's above my maximum allowable offer. But I tell you what—I can call my financial partner and see if he can sharpen the pencil a bit for us. Again, I'm not completely sure an increase is possible, but I'll do my best.
>
> Before I make that call though (because I don't want to waste their time), if we were able to get our offer up to [amount], would you say yes to that?

Notice how Chad exchanged the potential of an increased purchase price for a commitment to sign the contract right there? He also said he needed to check with someone to confirm. Negotiations can be easier if you operate under the illusion that there is a higher authority with a red line, whether it's a manager, partner, owner, or lender. You don't want the seller to think you have the final say on the offer. You are their friend, not the villain.

#9: Sign the contract.

This is the hard part, right? Well, no actually it isn't.

If you've done everything on this list—built rapport, set the frame, determined potential objections, and discussed numbers—getting the seller's signature should be *easy*. It should feel almost effortless at this point.

#10: Set expectations for what will happen next.

When you leave the house, it is critical that you and the seller are on the exact same page. Don't leave the appointment with the seller thinking, *We signed the contract, we'll close in two or three weeks, and this is a done deal.*

If you're going to wholesale the property, you'll need to let buyers see it. If you're a flipper, you'll probably need contractors to walk through to confirm your estimates. If you missed some critical repairs, you may not have a deal. Make sure the seller knows that someone will be doing walk-throughs.

#11: Send the contract to your title company.

Once the seller signs the contract, immediately send it to the title company and open escrow.

Make sure that the title company you use understands your business model and that some of your deals will inevitably fall through. Good title companies don't require you to pay for transactions that don't get closed, but they also may get annoyed if you consistently drop or cancel contracts with them.

Having said that, as a wholesaler, it's necessary to start processing the title immediately in case you have a buyer who wants to move forward right away. Most of the distressed transactions we do also have issues with the title, so if that happens to you, you'll have more time to work on it.

You'll need to strike a balance between being respectful to the title company and creating a quick transaction with buyers and sellers. In my experience, as long as you're clear with the title company about your business model and they know what to expect, the relationship will stay strong.

What If They Don't Sign The Contract?

When meeting with sellers in person, we close one out of every three or four appointments. Over the phone, we close one out of about every five or six. Your close rate will likely be lower in the beginning as you get the hang of the acquisitions process. This means you'll need to be prepared to leave meetings *without* a signed contract, and have a system to properly follow up with the sellers.

It's going to happen, but it's not the end of the world. Not every appointment turns into a deal, no matter how good your negotiation skills are.

What should you do when you can't get the contract signed?

Your goal should be to put yourself at the top of the list if and when the seller changes their mind.

We do this by leaving the seller with a list of questions to ask other real estate investors who might reach out to them. This is partly altruistic—not every investor has the seller's best interests in mind. But it's also a way to show the seller our experience and integrity. The questions function as a list of the benefits of working with our company.

Here are some of the questions we leave with sellers to ask other potential buyers.

- How many deals has the buyer closed?
- Can the buyer show you proof of funds?
- Does the buyer have referrals and testimonials from other sellers?
- Will the buyer show you pictures and addresses of past deals?
- Does the buyer have a website?
- Is the buyer Better Business Bureau approved?
- Can the buyer offer you personalized attention?

If the next buyer who comes along can't offer what we can, the seller is usually motivated to call us back.

These questions are designed to highlight my company's strengths, but they might not line up with yours. If you're a new wholesaler, you won't check all the boxes on this questionnaire. That's intentional—my most common competitors are new investors. As you create your own list of questions to leave with sellers, consider what will make you stand out from companies like mine.

In addition to the questions, you should leave additional information on a flyer or in a folder, including details such as the following:

- Who you are
- What you do
- Why your clients work with you (instead of a real estate agent)
- Testimonials from other sellers you've helped
- Your contact information

- Anything else that could help you stand out or set you apart

If the seller is seriously motivated to sell, but perhaps a stakeholder wasn't present or they want to wait a day or two to decide, Chad will leave them a range for the sale price. If other investors will be looking at the property, you don't want the seller to be able to say, "Well, Chad offered me $50,000—can you go higher?" Instead, leave them with a reasonable high and low number. Additionally, it's likely that the seller will call you back after they meet with those other investors to give you the opportunity to beat their offer.

If the deal doesn't work out, set another appointment for as soon as possible, ideally later that evening or the following day. This date should be concrete. An open-ended suggestion like "I'll call you tomorrow," or worse, "Call me after you've had time to consider" will make the seller less likely to meet with you again. Instead, say something like, "I'll be back on this side of town tomorrow at four o'clock. Can I stop by then?"

If the seller needs a month or so to decide, set a reminder to follow up with them later. People's circumstances often change. If you're setting up an automated follow-up system, write a general note that will automatically send to every seller you meet after a set amount of time. For example, you could automate a message to go out seven days after a meeting saying, "Mr. or Mrs. Seller, it was great meeting with you last week. Thank you for showing me the house. Are you still interested in selling it?"

To close one out of every three or four appointments like we do, follow-up is essential. Most sellers you meet won't be ready to sell right away, and deals fall apart for a variety of reasons. But with a good follow-up plan in place, you can keep reaching out to these homeowners and solidify yourself as their first choice when they decide they're ready to move forward.

Below are a few more tips to help your first appointments go smoothly.

Go to every appointment when you're starting out.

A lot of sellers will ask for full retail value when they first call you or when you call to confirm the appointment. Sometimes that might discourage you from visiting the property. But often things change once in-person negotiations begin. In our experience, many people ask for full retail only to drop it by 50% once Chad is there with them looking at the house. Donna was a perfect example of this. In the beginning, you also need the practice, so go on every appointment you can.

Dress casually and be yourself.

When you go on these appointments, just be yourself. Don't try to dress up or act differently than you normally do. Remember, these folks are already guarded and are looking for help, so they don't care too much about what the person who helps them looks like. They may also be embarrassed about the condition their house is in. They don't know what to expect and they don't know if they can trust you. Wearing a suit and tie or other formal attire might intensify these feelings. If you're comfortable, they'll be more at ease.

And speaking of comfort, don't forget to wear reasonable shoes. It's not uncommon to walk through tall grass, flea-infested rooms, or damaged areas. Chad wears a polo shirt, jeans, and tennis shoes to his appointments.

Be transparent.

If you're new, don't act like you've done 100 deals and certainly don't say that you have. Yes, you want to be confident, but you must also be authentic. I don't recommend volunteering that this is your first deal, but don't be afraid to figure things out with the seller together.

If you don't know something, say, "I don't know, but I'll call someone and find out." The seller will appreciate your honesty and will be glad to know that you care enough to do it the right way. Remember, if you can help solve the seller's problem and get the deal done with them, they don't care whether it's your first or your hundredth deal.

Show up early.

Early is on time, and on time is late. Show up to the appointment at least five minutes early and go to the door a minute before your appointment. It will set a professional tone for the rest of the conversation. But don't show up *too* early—you don't want to drop in on someone before they're ready for you.

If I'm doing a phone appointment, I punch the number in one minute before the scheduled time and hit Call right when it changes over to the exact appointment time. Sellers will appreciate that level of attention to detail, and will assume you will be just as professional when working on their transaction.

If you do need to show up late, let the seller know ahead of time. If you keep them waiting without resetting their expectations, they might see you as unprofessional and you could lose the deal just because of that.

Wholesaler-To-Investor Acquisitions

Acquisitions between wholesalers and house flippers can be much easier than direct-to-seller acquisitions. They *should* be easy—after all, everyone involved is presumably a real estate professional who understands how the deal works.

If you're a house flipper or landlord buying houses from wholesalers, here's a bit of advice to ensure your transactions go smoothly.

Remember that the wholesaler has earned their fee.

Some house flippers feel like they're the ones doing all the hard work and taking on all the risk. After all, if you're a flipper, *you're* the one pulling up old carpet and tearing out moldy drywall on a Saturday afternoon. You're the one paying for everything. You're the one who has to take ownership of the property and hold it for three to six months while it gets fixed up. You're working hard to earn every bit of the $20,000 you hope to make on the deal.

Meanwhile, the wholesaler just puts your name on the contract and walks away with a $15,000 assignment fee. How is that fair?

If you've read everything up to this point in the book, you know why it's fair. You know how much effort wholesalers put into finding the right sellers up front. From marketing to lead intake to seller negotiations, wholesalers do a ton of work to bring you great deals. By appreciating what a wholesaler does and not balking at their fees, you'll save yourself from the monumental task of finding these homes yourself. Instead, you'll get to enjoy mutually beneficial transactions for years to come.

Run your own numbers.

If the wholesaler you work with is an experienced professional, they'll have already factored your profit into their contract price with the seller, leaving you room to make money on the deal. In theory, all you should have to do is double-check the key numbers, like ARV and cost to repair, and complete a thorough walk-through to make sure they didn't miss anything critical.

However, you should always run your own numbers on every deal. Walk through the property, pull your own comps, and come up with your own ARV and repair estimates. Experienced wholesalers will be pretty good at crafting deals that work for everyone involved (yourself included), but no one is going to get it right every time. It's up to you to be sure the investment is profitable based on how you do business. Remember, everyone will come up with different MAOs based on their purchase, holding, financing and closing costs, their renovation costs, and their desired profit.

Don't be a pain to work with.

Have you ever wondered why wholesalers don't just flip the houses themselves? After all, once they have a house below market value under contract, couldn't they get an even bigger payday by doing the renovations on their own instead of assigning the contract to a flipper?

The answer is yes, they could. But wholesalers need to focus on marketing, negotiating with sellers, managing the transactions, and finding the next deal. They don't have time to manage contractors and oversee extensive renovations that could take months. This means that what the wholesaler needs from you, the flipper, is a *fast and simple transaction.*

If you're a pain to work with, or if you drag your feet, create issues, or become a hassle for the wholesaler, you're directly slowing down their business. If you're in the habit of constantly haggling with wholesalers or nitpicking their prices, they may just stop offering you deals and move on to someone who's easier to work with.

This doesn't mean you should give every wholesaler everything they want. But if you want to get deals from them, you have to be someone they want to work with. Wholesalers who do a high volume of deals will have rules in place that you need to follow. For example, my company expects flippers to put down a non-refundable deposit. Some flippers refuse to do this, so we don't do business with them. Simple as that.

This also means that if you place an offer, you'd better follow through with it. Experienced flippers will tell you that sometimes they make an offer, then realize they missed something—like a cracked foundation or a miscalculated ARV—but they buy the property anyway. Wholesalers will tell you the same thing. As a wholesaler myself, when I make a mistake, I'll often sell the house at my own expense. A career-long relationship is worth more than one deal.

When meeting with wholesalers or walking properties, make sure to show up on time with financing secured and ready. Flippers who do this then make an offer, follow through with it, work diligently with the title company, and always have money available for fast transactions are the ones wholesalers will keep working with again and again.

When I get a list of offers and company names bidding on a property, I remember the ones who gave us trouble in the past and those who are easy to work with. I've taken less money for a property in order to make that transaction easier on myself and my team.

Don't be afraid to make an offer.

This is probably the most overlooked tip when working with wholesalers. Often house flippers or landlords will see a wholesale deal and spend time running their own numbers or inspecting the property, only to discover that the wholesaler's asking price is too high to make the deal work.

When this happens, don't just walk away.

You've already invested time and effort to research the deal. Go ahead and make an offer anyway. Even if it's lower than the wholesaler's asking price, you don't know how much wiggle room they have. You also don't know what other offers the wholesaler is getting—they might be even lower than yours. You might be the only investor to submit an offer at all. So go for it!

In short, if you want to be a house flipper or a landlord wholesalers love to work with, remember these four things:

- Show up on time to all meetings and showings.
- Have financing available and ready to deploy.
- Don't over-negotiate the price.
- Don't back out of deals.

> **FLIGHT PLAN HANDBOOK: Practice Negotiating**
>
> Practice negotiating with everyone, everywhere. Negotiate terms on what you'll cook for dinner or how long your kids will watch TV. Use tactics like labeling and mirroring with friends and family. The more you practice, the more comfortable it will feel.
>
> Some great places to do this are new and used car lots, mechanics, retail stores and outlets, cell phone providers, and insurance companies. And of course, use your new superpower for good!

Everything I've covered so far—from knowing your WHY to the real estate ecosystem to marketing strategy—is critical to your success. Without this knowledge, you wouldn't get far as a new investor. But I am also willing to bet that even if you found everything you've learned so far to be helpful (even motivating), something has been nagging you this whole time. Looming in the background, ready to upend your plans. I know what you're thinking.

"How the heck am I going to get funding?"

Chapter 13
Funding Sources

It's time to talk about money.

Uh oh. This is the scary part, right? Where I drop the bomb and tell you that you've got to have $100,000 sitting in the bank before you can even think about flipping a house.

Wrong. You don't need to use *any* of your own money to flip houses or buy rentals.

To be clear, it *does* cost money to invest. You've got to buy the house, hire contractors, and pay for materials, inspections, down payment, closing costs, interest…you get the idea. This stuff adds up fast.

But you don't have to use your own money for any of it. And you don't need to have good credit, a cosigner, or huge cash reserves either.

> **A Quick Note**
>
> If you're a wholesaler, you might think you can skip this section. But this is important for you too. If you have capital available, you can double-close your wholesale deals, which is a great way to streamline the closing process. Whatever your real estate investing strategy is, you must have access to funds in order to be successful.

There are numerous ways to get all the funds you'll ever need to flip all the houses you want. But before I talk about *how* to get the money, let's figure out *how much* you'll need.

To do this, answer the following questions:

- How many houses do I want to flip this year?
- How much will each house cost to buy in my market?
- How much will it cost to renovate them?
- How long will it take to complete the repairs and get the houses sold?

Let's say you want to flip just one house, and it will cost $150,000 to purchase and $20,000 for repairs. Depending on how hot your market is, you'll need to estimate your holding costs. For this example, let's assume that you estimate the property will take two months to fix up and sell, and your holding costs will be about $1,000 per month. Then you'll have closing costs when you sell the property, which can end up being about 8% of the sale price. If the home sells for $215,000, closing costs will come out to about $17,200.

Altogether, you'll need $189,000 to flip this house. And that's on a low-cost deal with no buffer for unexpected expenses.

> Review Chapter 11 to see how I came up with these numbers.

You *might* have that much sitting in your bank account right now. But most potential investors don't, and this is precisely what stops them from getting started. When I started flipping houses, I didn't have that kind of money lying around either.

And if you want to flip more than one house every six months or so, you're going to need even more capital to work with. Only you know your personal goals. I can't tell you exactly how much funding you'll need. But if you want to build a thriving business flipping houses, you'll need to do more deals in less time—which means finding even more money. So let's talk about how you can get it.

> **Note:** Before I start talking about money, I want you to know there are lots of SEC (Securities and Exchange Commission) laws governing how you raise capital and use other people's funds for investments. Nothing here is meant to be legal advice or constitute an offer or solicitation for your money. Research relevant laws before you begin doing business. Make sure you're covered.

Funding Sources

There are three main funding sources I use when flipping houses—friends and family, private lenders, and hard money.

Friends And Family

You might be surprised how many people you already know who have money sitting around making little or no return. If you could offer them a consistent, secured investment paying between 4% and 6% interest per year, many of them would jump all over that opportunity.

Real estate investing is historically safer than the stock market because it's secured by an actual asset—the property. It offers much higher returns than CDs or high-yield savings accounts. You would be doing your friends and loved ones a favor by putting their money to work, and it's not hard to do. In many cases, you would only need a single document to set up this investment option.

Maybe you don't have the stereotypical rich aunt who's always traveling to exotic places or buying fancy cars. But chances are there are more people than you realize in your immediate network who could invest with you and help fund your deals.

Private Lenders

Private lenders are typically individuals who are already investing in real estate or are savvy investors in the market. Like I mentioned above, real estate is a great investment option for people with money—it's secured to a property and often comes with better rates than other options. Not only that, real estate has a cool factor that's appealing to a lot of people, especially since TV shows and media have made home purchases and flips popular.

Many former house flippers and wholesalers prefer to passively invest their money in other people's deals. Many private lenders are retired or simply looking to diversify their assets.

Hard Money

Hard-money lenders specialize in lending money to house flippers and other real estate investors. These folks will charge you much higher rates than you'll get with family and friends or from private lenders, but hard money is always available, fast, and fairly easy to get.

Your credit score isn't really a factor. What matters is the deal itself. Hard-money lenders will want to see the ARV, comps, repair budget, and other numbers before approving the loan.

In most cases, hard-money lenders won't loan the entire amount needed to purchase and renovate the house. They'll expect you to bring anywhere from 10% to 25% of the total costs yourself. This is called the **gap**, and many house flippers work with private lenders or friends and family to cover it.

Hard money is a great option when you're first getting started, because the lender will review the deal and give you their feedback on whether you've got your numbers correct before moving forward, which can be enormously helpful. It's also a good option when you're trying to scale your business, as you can tap into a lot of money quickly and use your other private funds to cover the gaps as needed, letting you do more deals at the same time.

But this flexibility comes at a cost—hard money often comes with a 12% interest rate or higher as well as some fees. Keep this in mind when you're running the numbers and pricing out your deals.

Notice that I didn't include conventional mortgage loans or banks on this list. That's because it's typically not possible to use conventional financing like Fannie Mae- or Freddie Mac-backed loans to flip houses. As a landlord, I highly recommend looking into the delayed financing exemption to do a cash-out refinance after you fix up and rent out your property. It is also possible to use local and regional commercial lenders to finance your flip projects, but that is beyond the scope of this book.

> I worked for about two years to create special relationships with national hard-money lenders LendingHome and Anchor Loans. I've used them on countless projects and negotiated a 100% funding deal with them for members of our 7 Figure Runway and 7 Figure Altitude mastermind groups. Our members can borrow 100% of the purchase and 100% of the repair costs for the houses they flip—no gap funding and no down payment required. That means there's no financial barrier whatsoever for the flippers in our groups.

How To Raise Private Money

So how do you actually get people to invest their money with you? Here are a few quick tips to help draw potential investors out of the woodwork.

- **Talk about what you do all the time.** Most real estate investors do this anyway. Post on social media, talk among your friends, share the books you're reading and the deals you're working on. Explain why you love flipping and wholesaling houses. Share what you're learning and what you've accomplished. As you educate the people in your network about real estate, they'll eventually start to see it from your perspective, and once they do, they'll be begging to lend you money because they'll understand what a powerful investment opportunity you're offering.
- **Explain the benefits of investing with you.** Once someone is interested in lending, give them a single-sentence elevator pitch.
  - If you're a flipper, this might sound like, "I help other people grow their passive income and net worth through investing in real estate with me."
  - If you're a wholesaler, maybe you'll use my favorite line: "I'm a real estate day trader."
- **Emphasize the long game over the short game.** If a person invests with you, they'll have the opportunity to make money for the long term by keeping their money with you year after year. That means you'll always have capital on hand to do your next deal, and then the next and the next. Make sure they understand that this is your goal and how it directly benefits them.

  Additionally, if you take care of them, they will want to keep their money with you for a long time. I've started to pay back some of my lenders recently, and they are actually pretty upset about it—they don't want to put it back in the stock market!

The bottom line is, you've got to put yourself out there. Get passionate about real estate and make sure everyone around you knows it. House flipping is cool and fun! Wholesaling is intriguing! Real estate investing is amazing! People want to hear about this stuff. The more excited you are, the more they'll want to go on the journey with you. Sometimes the money lenders feel like they are flipping houses too when they invest in your deals.

Attracting potential investors online has been a huge success for me. The first year of my business, I found most of my investors through organic Facebook posts. A carefully crafted social media presence is a great way to establish yourself as an influential real estate investor in your area, as well as giving you a ton of credibility. You can also raise money from podcasting, LinkedIn, or even YouTube videos. You could start a local real estate Facebook group or a create a local meetup or real estate investing club. Networking at investor events is another great place to meet potential lenders. They are everywhere.

My lenders include high school and college friends, family members, pilots from my previous Navy squadrons, airline pilots, and my dentist. You can also find lenders by joining existing online groups like my Private Facebook group. You can find the link to join in your Flight Plan Handbook at 7FFHandbook.com.

You can use a list provider to find potential private lenders who are currently investing their money in projects. The lenders you'll find there may charge you higher rates than you could get from friends and family, but it's a great resource, and they typically already know what they are doing and can act quickly if you have a good deal.

> I created a free training video that walks you through exactly how to use a very popular list service to find private lenders. You can find the link in the Flight Plan Handbook at 7FFHandbook.com.

Meeting With Lenders

After you've connected with a potential lender, it's time to meet and discuss the terms of their investment. It's critical that you go into this meeting with the mindset that this is a mutually beneficial arrangement. The lender is not doing *you* a favor; you are doing *them* a favor, by giving them a secured investment with a higher-than-average return. You are not asking for a loan; you are providing them with an opportunity!

You are not desperate. You are not looking for a handout. Your goal should be to radiate confidence, competence, and professionalism.

Before meeting with a potential lender for the first time, practice on friends and family. (But don't be surprised if they also want to invest with you after they hear the opportunity!) Get comfortable and confident in what you can offer. I treat every one of these conversations as a financial consultation, not a sales pitch.

After meeting with a private money partner, you should be able to answer these questions.

- **Where is the money coming from?**

    If the money is coming from their emergency savings and they're going to need it when their home floods, you don't want it. Remember, this money could be attached to a property for the duration of your hold time. If your lender might need the money back because a tree fell on their roof, you could have a big problem. You are looking for money that is outside of an emergency fund or day-to-day expenses. This could be investment funds they have in the stock market, excess money sitting in a savings account doing nothing for them, or (my favorite) capital in a retirement account like an IRA or 401k.

Pro Tip: Educate yourself on self-directed 401ks and IRAs—these are accounts that the lender likely won't need access to for a long time, making them good sources of funding for your real estate deals. Many people likely don't even realize they can use their retirement accounts to invest in real estate with you.

- **What return are they making on the money right now?**

  Ask them what their current return is on their accounts, then show them how you can beat that. Don't just offer them something like 8% or 10% right off the bat—you might end up paying way more than you need to. Let them tell you what they're currently earning first.

  If their rate is low, offer them a better rate, but don't overdo it. For example, if someone is making 3% and you offer 12%, they might think you're scamming them. But if instead you ask whether they would be interested in making 6%, plus the added security that real estate provides, they'll probably love you for it.

  When they tell you their current rate of return, you can ask, "What rate would you be happy with?" Maybe you can even double it. The word *double* gets people excited. And that could mean going from a 2% CD to a 4% return in your real estate deal.

- **How much can they lend right now?**

  Sometimes the person can only lend a small amount. If that's the case, you may find that they aren't the best option. It's more difficult to manage multiple small lenders than to work with one or two larger ones. Try to find a single private lender who can cover the full cost of the home purchase and renovations. If this just isn't possible, try combining the private lender's funds with a hard-money loan to cover the gap, or you could bring other investors together to fund one project.

- **What is the turnaround on their funds?**

    Where is their money now, and what is the timeline they would need to turn that around and invest in your deals? If they are moving their money out of the stock market, they may need a few days to sell their portfolio and transfer it out of that account. If it's in an IRA or 401k that isn't already with a self-directed custodian, that process could take up to 45 days before it's available. Additionally, it may take some time for them to get comfortable with you or the idea of investing in real estate, so you may need to have multiple conversations before they are ready to pull the trigger and send the funds.

- **What are their short-term and long-term goals?**

    This has to be a win-win situation. If you can't help your lender meet their goals, this won't be a good partnership. Find out why they called you and what success would look like for them this year and years to come if they decide to work with you.

Once you have this information, you can start to discuss the terms. Think of these as a system, where if one lever is moved in favor of the lender, another one must be moved in yours.

For example, if the lender wants monthly payments rather than annual or a balloon payment, you might negotiate a 6% return instead of 8%. Below are just a few of the levers you can discuss and tweak as needed.

- **Interest Rate:** This is the return percentage they'll receive on their investment. It is typically an annualized interest rate. You want the lowest number possible while still making the investor happy.

- **Payment Schedule:** When do they need to receive payments? Will it be monthly, quarterly, or a balloon payment? I prefer a balloon payment where I can repay principal and interest at the end of the project. Why? Because pretty much every flipper is on a cash flow roller coaster. Not having to pay out monthly or quarterly interest payments can help cushion the lean times. Also it allows you to pay back the lender from the project proceeds (instead of your own pocket).

- **Secured or Unsecured:** A secured investment is one that has a promissory note and a mortgage or deed of trust (depending on your state). An unsecured investment is one that is simply done on a promissory note and isn't secured to a property. There are benefits for you and your lenders on both, so depending on how you structure it, you could save money and hassle to make it a win-win for each of you.

> There is more information on secured and unsecured investments in my $500K Challenge, which is mentioned in the Flight Plan Handbook.

- **Timeline:** How long do you have to pay back the loan? This could be a year, six months, or less. You will typically want as long as you can get to pay it back, with no prepayment penalty if you are done early.

What if the lender demands outrageous terms?

Sometimes lenders will want 15% or more when you first talk to them. I have a special tip for when this happens. It's helped me get lenders from enormously high interest rates and poor terms to half of what they were asking initially. Here's what I say:

> Okay, I can understand why you would want to make 15% interest. Here is how I support my lenders to make sure their money is working as much as it possibly can for them.
>
> I keep a list of lenders I work with and the rates and terms they are looking to get with us. Some want 6% interest, and we use their money every day of the year. Then I have lenders who are looking for higher rates, like you. They are on the list, but their money isn't working with us much throughout the year.
>
> When a deal comes along, I simply go down the list from the lowest rate to the highest until I have all the deals funded. If it's okay with you, I'll put you down at 15%, but right now that will put you at the bottom of my list. I may or may not call you in the future to use your money. If you change your mind and go to 8%, I'll be more likely to. If you'll accept 6% with a balloon payment on the end, I'll make you money for as long as you're willing to lend it.

Of course you don't have to use this script verbatim, but it has worked magic for me over the years and I highly recommend it! Remember all those tips you learned in the last chapter too. Labeling, mirroring and Socratic questioning aren't just for sellers.

We work so hard to find these deals and negotiate with the sellers, so why would we just lie down for our lenders and pay them outrageously high interest rates with poor terms? Remember, you have the opportunities in today's market, and you are inviting them to come along on this money-making train with you!

Keeping Good Lenders

You work hard to find these lenders, but the real magic is in keeping them. Believe it or not, they have more money available than they told you on that first call, I can promise you that. Keep your lenders updated on the project they are involved in and your business as a whole. If a lender ever has to contact you to find out how their project is going, you likely aren't doing a good enough job of keeping them informed.

With that said, not every lender is going to want to hear from you frequently. During the terms meeting, find out how often they would be interested in getting an update—weekly, monthly, quarterly, or yearly. Maybe they'd rather not hear from you until you have money for them. Build out your system and train them to use it. If a lender says to report in daily, that should be a red flag that they are a potentially high-maintenance investor.

I encourage you to send a quarterly newsletter to all your lenders and potential lenders. Include details such as the size of your team, the number of deals you did that quarter, the average return, and your future goals.

We started out years ago by giving smaller, more individualized updates monthly on projects. However, the monthly updates got to be too much, so I told everyone to check out our company Facebook page to get the real-time updates on their projects and paid someone to do monthly walk-throughs of each flip we were doing. We now communicate with our investors quarterly.

The key is to set what works for you and train your lenders to that.

If you find a lender you enjoy working with, do everything you can to keep them around. Consider sending them thank-you notes or gift baskets after each project is complete. Go out of your way to show you care and that you appreciate working with them.

Don't ever stop looking for private lenders. Securing funds isn't something you do once and then forget about. I'm constantly looking for more money partners, and I recommend you build this into your business as part of your typical workweek. Reach out to and meet with as many people as you can. You never know who will fund your next project.

Right now, you might be desperate for a lender and willing to take whatever comes your way. However, I encourage you to approach lenders with the same determination you had for finding a great deal. Remember that you are providing your lender with an opportunity.

> ✈ **FLIGHT PLAN HANDBOOK:**
> **Raise $500,000 In 30 Days**
>
> Write down the names of a few family members, friends, and acquaintances who you think might be interested in diversifying their assets. Do you know anyone who is an active investor? Write their name down too. These are the folks you'll talk to.
>
> If you're serious about getting all the funding you need for your next deal and beyond, I'd like to invite you to check out my 30 Days to $500K Challenge.
>
> It's a 30-day program with daily videos where I walk you through the exact funding process I've used to raise over $12 million in private money over the past few years. I give you assignments and action steps and show you what to say and who to talk to for the best results.
>
> Anyone can join, whether you're an experienced real estate investor or you're new to all of this. Sign up in the Flight Plan Handbook or at 500KChallenge.com!

You'll spend the rest of your career meeting and negotiating with lenders. At first, it can be really intimidating. If you're nervous to strike up a conversation with a stranger, try practicing on your loved ones. Once you can answer their questions, graduate to your friends. As soon as you're comfortable explaining to strangers what you do, you're ready to meet with lenders.

If you're a flipper, your next critical step is the part that everyone imagines real estate investors do all day every day: renovations! In the next chapter, I'll teach you how to handle them the *right* way. And for all those wholesalers out there, it's worth your time to understand the basics of renovations. Doing so will make you much better at estimating repair costs and working with flippers in general. And of course, if you ever struggle to assign a contract, you'll need an exit plan. So even if you never intend to pick up a hammer, this section is still for you.

Chapter 14
Smart Renovations

Tyler Jensen lost $37,000 on the first house he flipped. It was borrowed money—he had taken out loans to buy and renovate the house, but he had bought it for too high a price and the repair costs had gotten out of control. He had to take out another loan to pay off the first one.

On the next house he flipped, he made $38,000, but it took months to complete. Long, grueling days where he doubted himself and wondered if he was just flushing more money down the drain.

On his third flip, Tyler made $70,000. By that point, he felt more confident. "We started getting better at flipping. We found better contractors. I got better at project management. I was talking to contractors, raising money, making phone calls all day."

He was building momentum. It was exhilarating. Tyler loved it. He was waking up at 4:00 AM every day, eager to manage multiple flips at the same time.

He joined 7 Figure Altitude and streamlined his business. Soon he made money on every deal, flipping more than 20 houses per year.

From the outside looking in, it seemed as though he had it all figured out.

But Tyler wasn't satisfied. Throughout all of this, the sticking point was always the renovations. It was the one part of the process that seemed to drag and where issues kept cropping up. He knew there had to be a better way.

One afternoon, while looking over a project plan with his general contractor Jeffrey, Tyler said, "What if we could flip a house in seven days?"

Jeffrey laughed. "Sure, if it's just carpet and paint."

"No, I'm talking about a full renovation," Tyler said. "Like the ones we've been doing. Kitchens, bathrooms—everything."

"You want to take a two-month renovation and do it in seven days? That's not possible."

But Tyler couldn't let the idea go. He thought about it more over the coming weeks and tried to imagine how it could work.

He looked at their usual renovation process and calculated how much actual time each subcontractor typically spent at one of their properties. It was always less than seven hours. If they could stack the contractors and coordinate everything perfectly, while minimizing wasted time by providing meals on-site and having all materials delivered in advance, it *could* be done. Tyler was sure of it.

He convinced Jeffery to try it. And on their next house, they did.

They bought the house on a Thursday. It was a three-bedroom, two-bathroom home. Tyler and Jeffrey spent Friday, Saturday, and Sunday walking through the house, planning every detail of the renovation. They went to Home Depot and bought all the materials. They even bought all the tools that would be needed and stored them on-site so no one would have to leave to get anything.

On Monday, the countdown started. Rain poured all week long, and through the storm, Tyler and Jeffrey and their team worked feverishly.

In the end, they didn't finish it in seven days.

They finished it in six.

On Sunday, the seventh day of renovations, the rain let up. Tyler brought a barbecue grill to the job site and cooked burgers for the team. Jeffrey brought a hammock, hung it between two trees in the front yard, and enjoyed the first sunshine after a week of bad weather.

It was the start of a new era for Tyler's house-flipping business. He and his team now flip 40 houses per year, many of them in less than a week. Some projects still take longer, but they've got the renovation process nailed down (pun intended).

I don't know anyone else who consistently rehabs their properties in one week. In real estate, this timeline is unheard of. Even for experienced house flippers, a full renovation usually takes four to six weeks at least.

So what's Tyler's secret? It comes down to two things—planning and people.

Creating A Scope Of Work

Tyler and Jeffrey spend just as much time planning as they do rehabbing. And with the right contractors, you can do in seven days what would take other investors months. The end result: you save time and money, which goes right to your bottom line.

The plan is outlined in a document called the scope of work (SOW), which Tyler describes as the "recipe of the flip." The SOW includes details like these:

- Cost of the work to be done
- Timeline to complete the work
- Milestones to be achieved at various intervals
- Tasks that are in-scope and out-of-scope

Here's how Tyler and his team create their SOWs.

1. Tyler's project manager does the initial walk-through.
2. He'll call their acquisitions team and say something like, "We can flip this for $35,000. Should we go for it?"
3. The acquisitions team responds based on the as-is value, ARV, and MAO. The budget has now been set at $35,000.
4. They buy the property, and the clock starts ticking.
5. Tyler's team—usually including a real estate agent, designer, and a contractor—does a second walk-through.
6. They agree on what needs to be done to achieve the highest ARV, like knocking out walls, adding a bedroom, or replacing kitchen cabinets. The contractor will offer insight into which improvements are the most cost-effective and which are feasible. The agent will make suggestions as to what homeowners are looking for. Together, they'll decide what the project will look like. The designer then makes a plan and takes it to the project manager.
7. Based on information from the designer, the project manager estimates the timeline, budget, and materials.
8. Then the whole team reviews the SOW and makes needed adjustments, while also planning for hidden costs.

9. The project manager then hires contractors to complete the work.

Tyler looks for inexpensive contractors who are available immediately. But cost isn't the only consideration—if one electrician bids the job at $3,000, another at $2,600, and one at $800, the low bid is an indication that something is wrong. Maybe the contractor didn't understand the scope of work or is new and not experienced enough to price appropriately.

When Tyler hands his project manager and general contractor the finished scope of work, it's a lot longer than the example below. Here's a sample of what his SOW looks like for just one category.

DRYWALL

	Quantity/ Sq. Ft,	Material Cost	Material Total	Labor Cost	Labor Total	Total Cost
New hang, mud, tape	75	$15	$1,125	$17	$1,275	**$2,400**
Patch	30	$5	$150	$10	$300	**$450**
Retexture (per room)	5	$50	$250	$40	$200	**$450**
Dumpster	3	$225	$675	$400	$1,200	**$1,875**

You can find a detailed full SOW with all 17 categories in the Flight Plan Handbook at 7FFHandbook.com.

Notice that for each subcontractor, the expected quantity or square footage is specified, as well as material cost, labor cost, and total cost. When contractors know exactly how many ceiling fans are to be installed and exactly how much flooring at what price they need to source, there will be less drama once construction begins. If there is a problem—like if the $3-per-square-foot vinyl flooring you chose is out of stock—the contractor will be more likely to call you rather than make a decision on the fly.

Tyler is able to flip 40+ houses per year because he has a great team. But even if you *don't* have a team, you can still leverage others' expertise to come up with a detailed SOW. If you have a trusted general contractor, invite them to the initial walk-through to help determine the cost to repair and the kind of renovations that are possible. They might charge you $100 an hour, but in return you'll get a very clear idea of whether the deal is profitable.

Then ask your real estate agent and contractor to do a second walk-through so you can make more informed decisions about what changes you can make to increase the ARV. Incentivize the agent by agreeing to sell the property with them.

Next, ask your general contractor to give you a line-item quote, or get bids from subcontractors to get a solid idea of what it will cost to rehab. Based on these recommendations, you can budget for materials, build a timeline, and figure out which subs you'll need to hire.

Contractors and agents will do this extra work if you compensate them appropriately and if you set an expectation that they will consistently get decent-paying work from you.

A detailed, well-planned SOW will also help with project management later on. If everyone starts on the same page, the possibility of major miscommunications and increased costs decreases.

You can get as detailed as you want with your SOW, but the most important thing is that your project total is at or under your total budget, including a buffer of about 10% of your estimated cost to repair. If your project total is $40,000, allocate $4,000 to miscellaneous problems that will inevitably come up.

How To Get Good Contractors

Renovating a house can be incredibly complicated…or it can be a breeze. It all comes down to the contractors you hire. This is the people part of Tyler's winning equation.

Like I said earlier, the one thing you *shouldn't* do is try to complete the renovations yourself. You should either hire subcontractors and manage them directly, or hire a general contractor to oversee everything and get the project to the finish line for you.

Subcontractors handle specific specialties like…

- Carpentry
- Electrical
- HVAC
- Masonry
- Plumbing
- Roofing

The appeal of hiring subcontractors instead of a general contractor is that subs are cheaper—you won't have to pay the general contractor's markup or labor.

Hiring a general contractor, however, can save you a ton of time and headaches, and can ensure the project is finished on time and with professional attention to quality. More importantly, general contractors already know the best plumbers, electricians, and other subs. They also handle the drama that comes with managing 10 different team members under a tight timeline. When the painters can't work because the drywall isn't ready, or when the electrician can't finish because the tile grout isn't dry, a general contractor will organize all parties to get back on track.

A good general will be able to catch errors that a new investor might not even think to consider. If the home doesn't pass a building inspection, your project could be set back considerably, so having an experienced contractor at your side can save you time and trouble.

That being said, general contractors often manage multiple projects simultaneously. That means they aren't singularly focused on expediting your project, and instead are trying to ensure that all their projects are moving forward. If your superpower is project management and you have more time than money, it might make more sense for you to act as the general contractor by hiring subs yourself.

Either option is fine—subcontractors or general contractor. But just be aware of what you're getting into either way.

Mike Simmons, a 7 Figure Altitude member and extremely experienced flipper, will tell you there are a handful of factors that can make or break a flip. In his opinion, one of the biggest considerations in your success will be finding the right people to do the work. Your contractors must have integrity and skill. They must be easy to work with and communicate effectively with you and the other contractors.

Finding Contractors

The best way to find good contractors is to get referrals from other real estate investors. This isn't always possible, as active investors tend to keep their favorite contractors busy, but it's a good place to start. Network with other investors in your area and ask who they use. Take advice from those you trust as well. It's possible they are recommending a contractor because they aren't using them anymore due to their performance. So this can be a double-edged sword.

Mike recommends driving around and looking for contractors at job sites. Is there a site with a lot of activity? Does the crew look efficient? Find out who is in charge or obtain contact information from the vehicles parked on the street.

But don't just walk onto a job site without being invited. If you step into fresh concrete or get smacked with a two-by-four, you'll create a huge headache for the person you're hoping to work with (not to mention the one you'll have from the board). You can also look at completed flip projects on the MLS or other listing sites and, if they look well done, try to find out who oversaw the project.

You can find good contractors online at sites like Craigslist, Angie's List, and Thumbtack. Or you can walk into a Home Depot, Lowe's, or any other building supply store and ask the person in charge of ordering materials who they recommend. This person works with contractors regularly and can tell you who's consistently doing jobs and handling projects similar to yours.

You can also show up to a place like Home Depot or Lowe's at 6:00 AM and hang out around the Pro Desk to see who's buying materials. This is a great way to network with contractors and get referrals for subs.

To take this strategy a step further, find a contractor at Home Depot, pull a $50 bill from your wallet, and say, "I'll pay you $50 to open your phone and give me your best HVAC specialist right now." This makes it look like you have deep pockets, which can give contractors the impression that you're a good person to work for.

Ask great subcontractors for recommendations of other great subs. Ask your best electrician what drywall team they like working with, for example. No one will be a better judge of quality work and professionalism than someone who works with them regularly. Additionally, ask them who they *don't* like to work with and wouldn't recommend. Keep that naughty and nice list running forever, and just keep adding to it over time!

Contractor Ad Example

Here's an example of an ad Mike put out on Craigslist to find a good contractor.

> ### Licensed Contractor Needed For Whole House Rehab
>
> I am looking for a licensed contractor who has a crew that can begin work on my property in Indianapolis immediately. The house is vacant and needs top-to-bottom renovation. Windows, floors, paint, new kitchen and bath, wall and ceiling repair, and new siding.
>
> This is an investment property that will be resold upon completion. I also have additional properties that need renovation but would like to create a working relationship with a good contractor on this project before working on the next one.
>
> In order for you to be considered, I need verification of license and insurance as well as references before work begins.

Notice that Mike is looking for a whole crew rather than an individual contractor who can start work immediately. He gives an idea of what needs to be done so prospective contractors understand the scope of work. He adds that it's an investment property, which signals to the contractor that the work must be done quickly and at investment pricing. He also suggests that if this project goes well, the contractor could be hired again in the future. Mike asks for references, and he'll absolutely go to those properties and examine the work done.

Make sure you're clear about both the quality of work and the price you are looking for. You do not want the absolute best contractor. Why not? They often have the highest rates and provide a high caliber of artisanship that a first-time homebuyer doesn't need. Your two-bed, one-bath starter-home flip doesn't need the elite level of work done by someone who builds million-dollar vacation homes.

That being said, you do need quality work. If a potential buyer walks into a home and sees paint on the floor or tiles that aren't flush, they're going to wonder what other problems are hiding behind the walls.

Paying Contractors

Before you hire a contractor, you need some information. Ask for a line-item quote so that you know exactly what you're paying for. You'll also need certain tax documents, such as a W-9 so you can send them a 1099 form at the end of the year. You'll also want to see proof of licenses and insurance to ensure they are a licensed contractor. You can usually find these licenses on your county, city, or state website, and I highly recommend you do that even if they provide you with it.

Reviews are also helpful when hiring contractors. Get a list of their past clients and call them to ask how they did. I even ask those people if they know anyone else who has worked with the same contractor. I try to find people who aren't on the contractor's list of recommendations, since those are probably their favorite past clients who will likely have nothing but good things to say about them.

If you can get past the contractor's inner circle, you'll likely get more honest feedback. In one instance, a contractor gave me a list of recommendations. Instead of only contacting names on the list, I asked one of them if they knew anyone else who worked with them. On contacting this other contractor, I learned the real story. This person didn't do a great job—they failed to show up on time, leave the worksite clean and tidy, or complete the project within the agreed date. Bottom line? This person wouldn't work with them again. That is why you ask for a referral that is not on the contractors list!

As a flipper, you can't always offer the highest price for work. But you can offer recurring work with weekly payments that are always paid on time. Your contractors will love you for that, especially since many of them deal with clients who are unwilling or unable to pay.

Some unethical contractors will give you a low bid knowing they will upcharge you throughout the process to make more money. This is why it's good practice to get line-item quotes so you can figure out exactly why one contractor is cheaper than another.

Included in your contract, you should have your contractors sign a waiver and release of lien upon final payment. This document essentially says that after the contractor is paid the amount agreed upon in the contract, they will not pursue a lien on the property.

As you scale your company and start managing a lot of contractors, you might want to give new ones a packet with information and expectations. It might include the following details:

- **Quality Standards:** Outline the quality of work you expect for the finished product.

- **Change Of Scope:** Who should the contractor contact if they need to make adjustments to the project scope and how? The unexpected will happen, and they will need to know how to proceed.

- **Payment Terms:** When and how will the contractor be paid? Make sure they understand that they need to send an invoice to get compensated.

Never pay a contractor without an invoice. You need proof of work done in writing prior to making a payment. Without it, a contractor could claim that they were never paid for the work done and put a lien on the property.

Instead, on receiving the invoice from the contractor, pay the balance and then have the contractor sign a lien release waiver. Consider sending the contractor an in-house template they can fill out and return upon completion of work.

Mike and Tyler both recommend against paying by the hour. Instead, pay by the job.

If the job requires expensive materials, a contractor might ask for a down payment. If you're working with a general contractor managing the entire project, they may need materials for a new roof, cabinets, flooring, or windows, which could easily cost more than $40,000. Not every contractor will be able to handle that kind of overhead, and they may be extended financially with other jobs. If you're working with a young contractor who is just getting started, they might not be able to float even $3,000 worth of materials.

But don't just give someone you don't know $40,000 on day one. A good guideline is to provide a maximum of 15% of the total for a down payment. In the beginning, I prefer to have them go to get the materials and I pay for them directly through an account with Lowe's or Home Depot.

Alternatively, you can ask for a materials list, purchase them yourself, and have it all waiting at the job site for the crew. But buying the materials yourself is a lot more complicated than it sounds and takes time and effort. Some of the challenges you might encounter with this approach include the following:

- Unless your contractor gives you a very clear list of exactly what they need (sizes, brands, colors), you might order the wrong items and set the project back by weeks.

- Some contractors get contractor and bulk pricing, especially on items like lumber. Those discounts likely won't be extended to you.

- Do you really want to spend your time running to Lowe's? Your time is better spent finding deals, not searching for the right-sized fittings.

If you're starting out, the best option is to do your research, hire the right contractor, and don't give them a bid down payment. Let them shop for the materials, and then pay the vendor directly yourself. Or give them a maximum of 15%, ask for a materials list, and confirm that those materials are at the job site after purchase.

Managing Contractors

Whether you hire a general contractor or multiple subs, you'll need to manage the project closely when you're first starting out, especially with new labor. As you get to know your contractors and establish a strong working relationship built on trust, you'll be able to step back a bit. But at the beginning, plan to keep a close eye on everything.

Visit the job site frequently. A lot can go off the rails if you don't check in for a week—within that time, the crew could make a bunch of decisions that directly impact your bottom line without your involvement. To help keep everyone accountable, ask your contractors to send you photos of completed work daily or every other day.

Most general contractors can do a little of everything, like carpentry, roofing, painting, drywall, flooring, and tile work. But that doesn't mean that they *want* to do everything or that they should. Tyler recommends asking each contractor what kinds of work they enjoy doing in order to find the best fit for each job. If someone hates detail work, you don't want them tiling the kitchen backsplash, do you?

Aside from hiring the right people for the right tasks, another key element of project management is ensuring that each task is completed in the right sequence. Demolition such as tearing out walls or ripping up flooring must take place before windows are installed or tile is laid. The drywall has to be dry before the painters can get started. Hardwood floors should be sanded and refinished before cabinets can be set. You get the idea.

Materials And Finishes

Choosing the right materials and finishes for the job is a huge part of the renovation process. Over-renovating will eat into your profit, but under-renovating can make the house undesirable and difficult to sell. And unfortunately, there isn't a set standard for which materials and finishes work best—it varies depending on your local market and the house's ARV.

Stephanie Betters is a 7 Figure Altitude member who has completely systematized the materials and finishes for her projects. She and her husband Zach created a three-tiered system to help their contractors and project managers choose the right materials for each job.

- A-grade materials are for high-end flips, new builds, or additions. For Stephanie, anything with an ARV over $300,000 gets an A grade. These aren't true "high-end" homes but rather nice houses in desirable neighborhoods.
- B-grade includes midrange, first-time-homebuyer houses with an ARV below $300,000. These materials are good but not high-end.
- C-grade materials are rental quality, meaning the finishes and materials are low-cost and can take wear and tear.

After defining these three tiers, Stephanie created two different styles: farmhouse and modern. These styles dictate which finishes and fixtures are used in each house at each level. Next, she and Zach created material lists for each combination—like "C-grade farmhouse" and "B-grade modern." These lists include items like flooring, light fixtures, bathroom mirrors, outlet covers, appliances, doors, windows, and cabinets. Not only does each look and grade come with a clear, finite list of exactly what will go into each home, it also offers various options in case a specific product is on back order or out of stock.

I think their system is brilliant, and it has allowed them to automate the process of choosing materials for their flips. If you don't want your phone blowing up with contractor questions, having a clear list of materials and backup options is essential.

Set your standards and stick to them. If you choose to install the A-grade package in a home with an ARV of $250,000, you'll likely lose money simply because square footage, number of beds and baths, location, and current market trends do more to impact ARV than materials do. Stephanie suggests that if you want to push the market price, stick with the appropriate level of materials and instead pay a little more for high-quality work, cleaners, and staging.

> **FLIGHT PLAN HANDBOOK:**
> **Create A Scope Of Work**
>
> Use the SOW example in the Flight Plan Handbook to create your own scope of work. You can find it at 7FFHandbook.com.
>
> 1. Use sites like Home Depot to price materials.
> 2. Search online for common contractor labor rates in your area.
> 3. Consider the timeline of the project.
>
> You'll make a lot of changes to your SOW after your first few flips. But just because there will be some adjustments made doesn't mean you should enter the project without one. Remember, effectively managing your timeline to avoid delays and holding costs is how you'll hold on to the profit you earned by buying at a discount.

Many of the steps I've taken you through up to this point—negotiating the best terms with sellers, buying houses at a discount, raising funds in advance, not over-improving properties, renovating quickly—are meant to make this next stage easy. Get all that other stuff right, and dispositions are pain-free.

Chapter 15
Pain-Free Dispositions

Your ultimate goal as a house flipper or a wholesaler is to *exit your deals as quickly as possible*. How you do so will look different depending on whether you're flipping or wholesaling.

- As a wholesaler, you exit the deal by assigning or double-closing the contract to an investor buyer.
- As a flipper, you exit the deal by selling the house to a retail buyer.

Real estate investors refer to this process as a **disposition** because it's the point where they dispose of the property. It's kind of a weird term. It almost makes it sound like you're throwing the property away or something. But hey, I didn't come up with it.

So let's talk about dispositions and how to exit your deals quickly for the most profit possible.

Dispositions For Wholesalers

You've found a motivated seller. You've done the prework. You've gone on the appointment, built rapport with the seller, negotiated, settled on a price, and signed the contract. You've sent the contract to your title company or attorney to get the title work ordered.

What's next? It's time to find a buyer for your contract.

The dispositions process looks something like this:

1. Build your buyers list.

2. Market the contract for sale.
3. Show buyers the property.
4. Negotiate the price with the end buyer.
5. Collect a nonrefundable deposit or fee.
6. Assign or double-close with the title company or attorney.
7. Repeat.

Let's break down each step in detail.

#1: Build your buyers list.

Your buyers list is literally just a list of potential buyers—house flippers, landlords, developers, short-term rental owners, and other investors who are interested in discounted off-market properties.

Finding buyers isn't just part of the dispositions process; you can and should be looking for them and updating your list whenever possible. This will increase the price at which you can sell your deals and increase your margins dramatically.

There are a lot of ways to find buyers. The simplest method is to network at REIA meetings and other investor meetups. You can also join online forums and groups.

One pro tip that blew up my buyers list is to go into these local online groups and search for the @ sign. This will pull up all the posts where buyers have listed their email addresses (trying to get deals sent to them). When I went into the Nashville market, I was able to build a buyers list of more than 1,000 names just by doing this. (I actually hired a virtual assistant to do this for about $3 an hour.)

You can purchase a list of recent cash transactions from a data vendor in your farm area and contact each person on the list. You can send them a postcard using their mailing address, but skip tracing them and then calling or texting would be even better. Both of these strategies combined work extremely well. You can even contact real estate agents to ask if they know any investor buyers. Try searching for cash transactions on the MLS, and contact the agents who facilitated them. You can even call property management companies and ask if they'd be willing to connect you with any landlords in the area.

#2: Market the contract for sale.

Remember the photos you took when you met with the seller? Write up a description of the house, the area, the upside potential of it, then attach the photos, come up with your asking price, and send the deal to all the buyers on your list. Make it clear that what you're offering is the contract, and that you're not selling the house itself.

Don't price the contract so high that no one will be interested, but also don't price it too low so you don't make a profit. When calculating your MAO, you considered the buyer's cut. Look at this price again. Is there enough room in the contract for them to make a profit? The biggest complaint investors have about new wholesalers is that they price their properties too high.

The purpose of this email, text, and/or ringless voicemail that gets sent out to your buyers list is to entice interest in the property. Other investors should be chomping at the bit to get in there and buy it so they can make money. You have worked so hard to get this property under contract at the right price for all involved, so take your time to make this look good.

When you send the deal to your list, include the following details:

- Property address
- Estimated rental price
- Pictures and video, if you have them
- Square footage
- Number of bedrooms and bathrooms
- Lot size
- Year built
- Any other valuable info that makes the property a good deal

You may notice that I left out ARV and estimated repair costs. I used to include these in my marketing materials but stopped after a few years. Never in my years of doing this and hundreds of properties closed have I had an investor tell me that my ARV is too low or my repair costs are too high. But the opposite is certainly true, and my phone and email would blow up with complaints. So now I let the investors come up with their own ARV and repair costs based on their business model. This has worked out great for me—my phone and email are not as overloaded, and my deals still close.

I see a lot of new investors get caught up in the pricing of their properties and focusing on what they email the contract out for. Andy McFarland told me years ago, "The market will dictate the price of each property." At first I didn't get it, but over time I've seen that if I misprice it by a reasonable amount (let's say $5K too low), the market will correct it. This is precisely why we don't take the first full-price offer we get.

You may get buyers reaching out to you who you don't know personally. Maybe one of the people on your list forwarded your email to someone they know. In this case, make sure to vet them before moving forward. Ask them how many homes they're currently flipping or what their rental portfolio looks like. Find out how they pay for their deals. Request proof of funds if needed.

As a new investor, don't be intimidated to ask for these details. If you ever asked me for proof of funds, I would gladly oblige. Showing that you don't waste your time signals to serious investors that you won't waste theirs.

#3: Show buyers the property.

Be present when your buyers are checking out any property, whether it's owner-occupied or vacant. I always like to show a property to multiple buyers at the same time, as it creates a bit of an auction vibe, which encourages competitive bidding.

Show up early, before any buyers do. For owner-occupied properties, make sure that everyone else shows up at the same time so as not to inconvenience the homeowner. Make it clear before the showing that the buyers should not discuss any financial details with the seller. Most will happily agree to these terms because they want to do business with you in the future. Also, do not allow investors with five contractors in tow into the home if they aren't likely to buy. Respect the seller's home, your time, and the investor's time.

That doesn't mean you shouldn't work with someone who has never done a deal before—after all, this might be your first deal too. Especially in the beginning, you'll gain a ton of experience by showing a property as much as possible, especially if it's vacant. If your buyer is an experienced flipper, they may be able to give you feedback on your estimated cost to repair and help you get better at acquisitions.

#4: Negotiate the price with the end buyer.

If you're selling to another professional, this should be a high-level, fast-paced discussion. If you're selling to a future homeowner, you might have to use tactics from the negotiations chapter to expedite the transaction.

#5: Collect a nonrefundable deposit.

Once you've found and vetted an interested buyer, it's time to agree on a few details.

- **Close Date:** Does their timeline align with the seller's?
- **Contingencies:** We try to avoid allowing contingencies like appraisals and property inspections. We look for serious, experienced buyers who don't need them.
- **Payment Method:** Are they financing with cash, hard money, or something else?
- **Price:** This is usually set in stone—we don't send our deals to hagglers.
- **Additional Terms:** Are there any other terms and, if so, is the buyer aware of them and do they agree to them? This could include a tenant who is staying in the property or an escrow holdback. These items should be spelled out on the contract.

As with acquisitions, it's critical to agree on these terms as early as possible. Don't assume that a buyer will pay with cash and have no contingencies.

When wholesaling, we require a $5,000 nonrefundable deposit for contracts over $100,000 and a $2,500 deposit for contracts under $100,000, which secures the buyer's interest in the property, meaning we won't show it to anyone else or continue to market the contract for sale.

You might encounter resistance to a deposit like this. In my experience, anyone who isn't willing to pay your deposit falls into one of these categories:

- They can't afford it or they don't have any cash.
- They don't know what they're doing.
- They aren't serious about the property and will likely back out anyway.

To be clear, if the *seller* backs out, or we as the wholesaler can't get clear title, the buyer will always get their deposit back. The deposit is only in place in case the *buyer* refuses to buy the property after committing to do so, in which case we transfer a portion or all of the deposit to the seller for the inconvenience. If we have to go back out to our list to get the deal done with another buyer, the price will typically go down. We have had to close on properties last-minute because buyers backed out of the deal the day before closing, and finding the money a day before closing is expensive.

As a wholesaler, you are the face of this negotiation. If a buyer backs out, the seller doesn't think, "Wow, that buyer really screwed me over." On the contrary, even if you didn't do anything wrong, it will reflect negatively on you. By giving the seller a portion of this deposit, you can usually protect your reputation.

#5: Assign/double-close with the title company.

You can close a wholesale deal in two ways: assignment or double-close.

- **Assignment**

    If you recall, when you sign a purchase contract with a seller, it gives you the ability to purchase the property for the agreed-upon price. When you assign that same contract to another buyer, you're transferring your purchase ability to that person in exchange for a fee. The assignment allows the buyer to take over your contract.

    We do an assignment of contract whenever possible because it's the cheapest way to get a deal closed, requires none of our money, and puts the most money in the wholesaler's pocket.

    The wholesaler isn't selling the *property* to the buyer, because legally the wholesaler never owned it. Instead, the wholesaler is selling the *contract*.

> If you don't have an assignment agreement, you can download one for free from the link in the Flight Plan Handbook. This is the same agreement I've used on hundreds of deals. Treat it as a starting point, but find out whether this contract will be valid in your state before using it. Find the handbook at 7FFHandbook.com.

- **Double Close**

    During a double close, the wholesaler purchases the property themselves and then immediately sells it to the buyer minutes later. This method of closing a wholesale deal can be simpler and easier than an assignment because it's technically the same as a regular real estate transaction. There's no risk of the seller finding out that the buyer is paying you more than what you offered or the buyer seeing your wholesale fee in the middle.

    The only problem with double closing is that it requires you to come up with all the money to buy the property yourself. This is one reason it can be helpful for wholesalers to have access to capital, like I mentioned in the chapter on funding deals. There are also transactional lenders who will loan you money on an extremely short-term basis (think several days max) so you can double-close your deals.

You'll need to decide which option works best for you and for your sellers and buyers.

Title Companies And Transaction Coordination For Wholesalers

Many wholesale transactions, especially assignments, are a bit different from what the title companies are used to. As a result, some may not know how to handle an assignment. It's essential that you find a company that understands wholesaling.

If you contact a title company and explain what you're trying to do but are met with blank stares—or worse, accusations that what you're doing is illegal—move on to another and keep trying. Some are investor-friendly; others aren't. Start by asking around and getting referrals from other real estate investors in your area. This is how I've always found mine when I move into a new market.

If you are in a state that uses attorneys to close real estate transactions or you can use either, just interchange "attorney" with "title company" in this section.

Here are a few actions the title company will take.

- Process the contract.
- Run the title and background on the property.
- Look for liens, judgements, or late mortgage payments.
- Confirm the owner of the deed.
- Gather necessary signatures.

- Collect and distribute the funds.

What you *don't* want is for the title company to get involved in the negotiation process. You also don't want them to start contacting the sellers and buyers instead of you.

It took me a long time to find my transaction coordinator, Ashlea Detwiler. She is the best in the business because she can expertly communicate with sellers, buyers, and title companies. Ashlea tells our 7 Figure Runway and 7 Figure Altitude members that they must be clear up front about what they expect from the title company.

It's also important to send them your contract early so they can assess it. Are they comfortable with it? Do they need to make any changes or have their lawyers look it over?

> If you're looking for a title company, jump into my Facebook group (find the link in the Flight Plan Handbook) and ask. We can suggest national title companies, and there is probably a group member who can recommend a local company in your area.

Dispositions For House Flippers

Disposition is a little simpler for house flippers because it's almost completely hands-off…or at least, it *should* be.

Here's the disposition process for flippers.

1. Perform a final inspection.
2. Stage the property.
3. Photograph and list the property.
4. Negotiate with the buyer.
5. Close the sale.

You can pretty much sum this up as: "Make sure the house is finished, then list it with a real estate agent and move on to the next deal." Simple, right?

Unfortunately, many house flippers get too involved in the process. They try to cut corners and reduce costs without realizing that the longer it takes to sell the house, the more they're going to end up paying.

Don't fall into that trap. Here's a quick breakdown of everything you should be doing during the dispositions stage.

#1: Perform a final inspection.

Walk through the property after the contractor has confirmed that the inspection is complete. It helps to use what we call a punch-out list to make sure everything is cleaned up and finished off.

Here's Mike's punch-out list, which I suggest you follow.

- Make sure the trim is painted and that none of the trim paint is on the ceilings or walls.
- Check that all switches, like lights and garbage disposal, turn on and off.
- Make sure the outlets work by plugging in appliances or your cell phone.
- Check the plumbing by turning on all the faucets and letting them run to make sure everything is draining properly.
- Flush all toilets.
- Open, close, and lock all windows and doors to make sure they function properly.

- Hook up the appliances, including the refrigerator and stove. Wait for the fridge to become cold and the stove to get hot.
- Leave all appliance warranties in a drawer for the new homeowner.
- Make sure all contracts, including release of lien, are accounted for.
- Ask contractors to come back and fix any issues you've noticed.
- Pay all contractors in full for work done.

#2: Stage the property.

Yes, this costs a little bit of money—usually 1% of the sale price—but like I mentioned earlier, I recommend staging every house you sell. How you furnish and describe your property, the pictures you use, and the list price will all impact your profit in a big way.

Staging is a great way to increase the sale price of a home and sell it faster. When done effectively, it helps the buyer imagine actually living in the home. Without furniture, a property can look pretty sparse.

We stage just about all of our flips. But don't just take it from me. Terry Burger is a member of the 7 Figure Altitude group, an experienced house flipper, and a former real estate agent who used to sell 80+ houses per year. He recommends staging all high-end and midrange homes. The only time you can get away with *not* staging a house is if you're in a hot market with low inventory where you're getting offers right away before even listing it.

If staging still feels like an unnecessary expense, remember what I said at the start of this section: your goal is to exit the deal as quickly as possible. I've had houses sit on the market for months. It's not fun. It's the worst possible outcome. Spending a little money to accelerate the sale is worth it.

#3: Photograph and list the property.

Contact a real estate agent in your area to list the house. Agents usually make their money from a commission on the final sale price of the property. You may be able to save money by developing a close relationship with an agent who will lower their commission percentage in return for getting deals from you on a recurring basis. That said, you shouldn't shortchange your agent—they work hard to find buyers and facilitate transactions.

Terry says that if he brings an agent 40 deals per year, he expects them to take those at 1% commission or less. But a new house flipper can't ask an agent to give them this kind of deal when they're only bringing them a handful of properties a year. So if you're just starting out, keep this in mind as a cost-saving strategy to use in the future.

You can find flat-fee agents who will list the property on the MLS for a small fee without doing anything else to move the sale forward. With a flat-fee listing, you'll need to handle all buyer communication and negotiations yourself, which can get tedious and take up a good deal of time.

In my opinion, it's better to just stomach the agent's commission and allow them to work for you. A good agent can be worth their weight in gold. Even Terry doesn't list his own houses anymore. Do you want to spend time finding buyers and negotiating with them when you could be searching for your next deal?

Here are a few listing tips to maximize profit.

- **Hire a professional photographer.**

  High-quality photos sell houses—period. Don't cheap out on the photography or just crank out some blurry photos. In most markets, photographers only charge about $500, and it's one of the best investments you'll make.

- **Write a compelling description that tells a story.**

  On the MLS, everyone copies everyone else. Somehow, every single property is a "beautiful and spacious" three-bedroom with "gleaming" hardwood floors and "generous" bathrooms. But flowery language doesn't sell houses—it just comes across as amateur. Instead, tell the reader a story that highlights what makes the house special. Does it have a covered porch? Is it within walking distance to parks or downtown? Describe what makes the property charming or unique to potential buyers.

- **Don't use industry jargon or shorthand.**

  In your listing, avoid abbreviations like "2BD2BA." It's clunky and distracting. Keep the writing simple and free from industry jargon. You don't want the buyer to have to use Google to understand what they are looking at. Focus on what's important to buyers. Your agent can help you craft a compelling description.

#4: Close the sale.

Negotiation is just as relevant here as it is with the sellers, the lenders, and everyone else I have mentioned so far. Make sure your agent is negotiating well on your behalf.

Once you've accepted an offer, your real estate agent will handle the details. They will coordinate tasks like showings, inspections, and appraisals.

One final tip: stay objective. A buyer might say that they "don't like the tile" or that they think the roof isn't going to last much longer. An inspector might start nitpicking all kinds of minor details. Don't let it get to you.

Maybe you spent a lot of time and money upgrading the bathroom fixtures only for a buyer to call them "outdated" even though you know they're brand-new. Perhaps the buyer is claiming they're going to need to redo some of the work you've done because it doesn't suit their tastes, and as a result, they want a discount off the price.

It can feel frustrating or even infuriating to hear these comments, but keep your feelings out of it. This is a business transaction. It might make good financial sense to accept that buyer's lower offer so you can move on to the next house, even if you believe someone else should love the work you've done.

Your goal isn't to win the respect and admiration of your buyers, although it's wonderful when that happens. Your job is to make as much money as you realistically can while exiting the deal as quickly as possible and moving on to the next one. Stay out of the way and let the listing agent handle it. They can help as an objective party. And you should already be working on your next house.

That's the next step for both house flippers and wholesalers—step back, dust yourself off, take a deep breath, and *do it again*. Find the next deal. And then the next.

Before you know it, you'll be flipping or wholesaling five to ten houses per month like many of our 7 Figure Altitude members.

On the wholesaling side, if your deals are solid, it only takes four or five transactions per month to reach $1 million in gross profit per year. That's only about one per week.

On the house-flipping side, if your flips stay on time and under budget, it might only take two or three renovations per month to reach $1 million. That might only require two general contractors managing two flips each at a time, with a solid six-week turnaround per project.

You're already much closer to a seven-figure income than you might think. That is, if you're ready to take the leap.

Chapter 16
Take The Leap

You may be wondering what happened to Arianne and Chris. Back in Chapter 5, they were stuck with a couple of rental properties and didn't have the money to buy more. They were in a hurry to achieve financial freedom as quickly as possible so they could visit family overseas. I met them at an REIA meeting and told them about wholesaling. They were interested and eager to learn.

So how did they go from being eager to learn to earning $1 million in gross profit per year just two years later?

- They learned strategies that *actually* work, not rehashed guru nonsense.
- They followed the *Shuhari* principle (which I'll explain in a moment).
- They took *action*.
- And they *accelerated* their learning curve in a specific way that many investors ignore.

If you can do these four things, you can achieve your real estate investing goals.

What's Working—And What's NOT

If you've read this far, you understand how house flipping works and how wholesaling works. You've learned the fundamentals of real estate investing. But that is just the beginning.

Each topic has deeper layers to dig into. I could have written an entire book just on how to find deals, for example. Or on raising funds and connecting with private lenders. Really that could have been a whole series.

When I met Arianne and Chris at that REIA meeting, we talked about the fundamentals of wholesaling houses. But in our short time together, I knew we wouldn't be able to cover everything.

I told them about a three-day live event for real estate investors that I was helping put together called Flip Hacking LIVE. "Some of the best wholesalers and house flippers in the nation are flying out for this," I said. "They're going to walk through the exact strategies that are working right now. You should come!"

They had to pull some strings, but Arianne and Chris made it that year.

October 2016 was the first Flip Hacking LIVE ever.

Since then, we've held the event every year, and the information shared there has changed the lives of thousands of real estate investors.

Chris and Arianne took what they learned at that first FHL event and, in the 12 months that followed, they did more than 50 deals and brought in close to $800,000 in gross profit. In one year.

Flip Hacking LIVE is the highlight of my year. And maybe I'm biased, but I don't think there's any other event where honest, genuine real estate investors share exactly what they're doing in the trenches every day to close hundreds of deals per year—at least not at this level.

This was Step #1 for Arianne and Chris. It can be yours too.

> I'd like to invite you to join me at our next Flip Hacking LIVE event. We'll spend three days diving deeper into everything you've learned in these pages.

The *Shuhari* Principle

My oldest son Will started martial arts lessons. He's learning about a concept called *Shuhari*, which describes the stages of learning to master an art.

At first, in the Shu phase, you have to do exactly what the sensei says over and over and over again. No questions, no innovation, no changes. If the sensei says, "Punch," you punch. And then you punch again, and again, and again—until you've mastered every detail.

After a while, the sensei will add in some new concepts, maybe blocking or kicking. At this point you *still* aren't doing anything original. You're not developing a style or figuring out anything on your own. You're mastering the basics: basic punches, basic kicks, basic blocks. This is known as the Ha phase.

After a long, long time, you enter the Ri phase. This is about innovation. You create new strategies and moves, and eventually, you might even eclipse your sensei. But this takes many years—maybe even a lifetime.

This progression combines the three phases into *Shuhari*.

What happens when we apply this principle to real estate investing?

When I started wholesaling in 2016, I just did exactly what the other investors and my mentors told me to do. I didn't question it or try to figure out my own way of doing it. I saw their results, learned their strategies, and took action.

Arianne and Chris did the same thing. They came to Flip Hacking LIVE, learned what worked, saw how to do it step-by-step, and implemented without overthinking it.

After that, I was able to add in some new concepts and link different strategies together. I took elements of what I liked from various investors and created my Frankenstein model of a business. But I didn't create new processes or implement original strategies until I mastered the basics. That's when I started innovating and doing things no one else was trying. And I've seen so many of my 7 Figure Runway and 7 Figure Altitude members follow this same progression with massive success!

If you're new to real estate investing, keep the *Shuhari* principle in mind. You don't need to chase the latest cool real estate trend. Your goal should be to find one tactic that's already working and do as much of it as you can.

It's tempting to want to do a little bit of everything at first. But if you do, you will lose focus. The time will come when you can pivot into new business models, markets, or techniques. But remember that it's better to master one strategy than to do several poorly.

How My Library Card Almost Cost Me $600,000

I love books. I love them a little too much. And it almost cost me $600,000.

When I decided to start flipping houses more than seven years ago, I grabbed my library card, drove down to the library in Patuxent River, Maryland (where I was stationed at the time), and checked out a couple books on real estate investing.

These were good books written by experts. I couldn't wait to crack them open.

That night, after my wife Lucy was asleep, I sat down and started reading. At the time, I felt this was the best way to learn a new skill. After all, that's what I had done in college.

I figured all I needed to do was learn how to flip houses, and then I'd be able to go out and do it myself.

But a strange thing happened...

After I finished reading those two books, I didn't feel ready to start flipping. I had lots of unanswered questions in my mind that they hadn't covered.

So I went back to the library and got a couple more books.

I read them, and when I finished, I had even *more* questions.

I think you can see where this is going.

I did this for a year—checking out book after book on topics like investing and flipping so I could build a real estate empire. But it was never enough.

Anytime I decided to find a house to flip, I got cold feet. I wasn't sure where to start. I always thought, *If I just learn a little more, I'll be ready.*

Have you ever felt this way? It's commonly called analysis paralysis. And when I got started, I had it bad.

Looking back, it's easy to see what I was doing wrong. I was caught up in what I call the Lie of Knowledge. We're taught this lie from a young age. It's a big part of why so many people grow up to be employees rather than entrepreneurs. (Nothing wrong with either path, but our schools are clearly designed to push kids into one rather than the other.)

The Lie of Knowledge is simple:

The difference between success and failure in anything is how much knowledge you have.

But knowledge is only half the battle; the other half is implementation.

Don't get me wrong, you do need knowledge. But to succeed at something—especially flipping or wholesaling houses—you've got to have the passion, the energy, the mental clarity, and the drive to get out of your comfort zone and apply what you've learned.

These aren't attributes you can get from a book.

Yes, I know this might seem ironic, since you're literally reading a book right now. But my point is simply this: After you finish this book, the next step isn't to read another book, and then another and another. The next step is to *take action* and *implement* what you've learned.

I know a lot of wannabe real estate investors who have been hanging out on the sidelines for years. Maybe they've done a deal here or there. Usually they haven't started yet. But either way, they're stuck.

They read books…but don't apply anything.

They register for seminars…but don't attend because something "more important" always comes up at the last minute.

They buy online courses…but never actually watch the videos.

They go to REIA meetings…but sit in the back instead of actively networking with other investors.

They keep hanging out with the same small group of wannabes.

These guys and gals are smart. But if they would follow through and *implement*, they'd be unstoppable. Just like me eight years ago, they're missing that step.

So how did my library card almost cost me $600,000?

After I put the books down and got to work, the next year, I did 67 deals and made about $600,000 in gross profit. And that was just the beginning.

By the time I was talking with Chris and Arianne about wholesaling at that REIA meeting in Florida, my business was already well underway. Because I took action, I had the privilege of giving back to other investors by helping people like them take the next steps on their journey to financial freedom.

Accelerate Your Learning Curve

As Arianne and Chris's business started to take off, they intentionally leveled up their network by joining the 7 Figure Altitude mastermind group.

They came to meetings and met guys like Andy McFarland and Mike Simmons. They asked questions and dug into what other successful investors were doing. They learned what to do and what not to do. When they made mistakes or ran into obstacles, they had people to turn to who could encourage them and relate to what they were going through.

By getting around the right people, they skipped years of trial and error—and they scaled their business from two rental houses to 100+ deals per year within two years.

Today their business is bringing in over $1 million in profit annually. But even better, Arianne and Chris are able to take several months off every year and travel to visit family while their business keeps running without them.

This is true freedom.

It's the kind that lets me focus my time and attention on helping other investors through the 7 Figure Flipping podcast, the events we hold, the mentoring and mastermind groups we run, and more.

True freedom through real estate investing starts with learning the fundamentals and seeing what's possible. With shifting your mindset and recognizing the opportunity. With understanding *how* this business works. And I hope this book has done all of that for you. But it doesn't end there.

> If you're an active investor and you're ready to scale, consider becoming part of the 7 Figure Altitude group. It's not for everyone, but over the past few years, we've built a community that I'm so proud of—one founded on honesty, integrity, and abundance.
>
> You can learn more and apply to join at 7FigureAltitude.com.

You're starting a major journey, and it's going to be hard at first. Surround yourself with like-minded people who will not only give you practical advice but also lift you up when times get tough.

What Freedom Looks Like

Not long after I first met Arianne and Chris, I got some devastating news.

At the time, my wife Lucy was pregnant with our second son James. The pregnancy had been uneventful up to that point. I was still flying full-time for the Navy in Pensacola. My real estate business was growing fast. I had some money in the bank. And I had begun to hire team members to handle the day-to-day work of finding deals, talking to homeowners, and selling our contracts.

Then we got the news that James's heart wasn't developing properly.

The doctors ran more tests and discovered that he had a unique chromosome anomaly called Mosaic Ring 13 that had caused a heart defect.

His diagnosis upended our lives. Our complete focus was on him. How would we support him? How could we give him the best care possible? It completely altered the trajectory of my life and my family's future.

James would need multiple open-heart surgeries after birth. These operations and the weeks of intensive care associated with them would be grueling and extremely risky.

I started trying to find the doctors and medical facilities that would give him the greatest chance of survival. We settled on Vanderbilt Children's Hospital in Nashville, Tennessee.

With just a month left to go until James' birth, and only two weeks before that first Flip Hacking LIVE, I bought a house in Tennessee sight unseen with cash and moved my family there immediately. We met with doctors and started planning next steps for our son.

James entered the world right on schedule. Over the next six months, our tiny newborn son endured four open heart surgeries and three cardiac catheter insertions.

Of course, Lucy and I were there with him in the hospital for all of it. Week after week, month after month, I held his small hand. I saw him smile for the first time. I watched him sleep.

Through it all, my real estate business paid the bills.

I didn't have to worry about showing up to a 9-to-5 job. I didn't have an angry boss breathing down my neck. I didn't have to ration sick days or use vacation time to be with my son. I didn't have to beg people on the internet for money to cover the huge costs. We had all the money we needed to care for him and live in a comfortable home close to the hospital.

That's real freedom.

Today, James is happy and growing and full of energy. His story is part of my WHY. Just like Lucy and Will and our youngest son Lucas, he's the reason I built this business.

I've done all of this for them. And it has been hard, but so incredibly worth it.

As I wrap up this book, I want to leave you with one question.

What does freedom look like for you?

The path is laid out ahead of you. Are you ready to take the leap?

Bonus Chapter
Goal Setting

30/60/90 Goals

This might be the most important part of this book. And I've saved it for the end because it will directly impact what you do next.

You're about to set out on the next step of your real estate investing journey. But you won't get anywhere without *goals* and *accountability*.

Memorize this formula:

Goal Setting + Accountability = Measurable Results

Goals are great, but only if you know how to set them the right way.

Inside the 7 Figure Runway and 7 Figure Altitude mastermind groups, our members set 30-day, 60-day, 90-day, and yearlong goals. They take action on these goals and stay focused with weekly small-group accountability sessions. This is where the real magic happens!

Even if you don't have anyone to hold you accountable to your goals yet, you can still practice setting effective goals to push you forward.

How To Set SMART Goals

The SMART system was created by George Doran as a way to help people develop meaningful objectives. SMART stands for…

- Specific
- Measurable
- Attainable
- Relevant
- Time-Bound

Here are some thoughts on SMART goals for real estate investors.

Specific

Wishy-washy, generic goals are not motivating. Goals like "I want to make money" or "I want to flip some houses" are not going to get you where you need to go. Instead, set a specific goal like "I want to make $100,000 in the next three months" or "I want to close twelve deals by the end of this quarter." Without a specific goal, you have nothing concrete to hold yourself accountable to, and you won't know whether you've achieved it.

Measurable

Measurability goes hand-in-hand with specificity. You have to be able to measure your success, and therefore your goal needs a specific target to hit. Maybe you're thinking, "I want to grow my business." Fine. But by how much, and by what date? Make sure your goal is built around something quantifiable.

Attainable

Be realistic. Set a goal you can actually achieve...or at least get close to. Bill Gates and Tony Robbins are both credited with some version of the quote, "Entrepreneurs often overestimate what they can do in a year, but underestimate what they can do in ten." Set goals you think you can reach within the timeline you've chosen.

Relevant

Make sure your goal is worth striving for and that it aligns with your values. Look back at your WHY and compare that to each goal you set. Every goal should align with your values. If it doesn't, it's not going to move the needle for you or your business.

Time-Bound

There needs to be a shot clock on every goal—a time-based limit. Similar to the Attainable factor, your deadline should be challenging but not unreasonable.

Many successful people talk about the value of actually writing down your goals. When they are just thoughts in your head, it's easy to change them or forget about them altogether. It's easy to ignore them if you don't see them every day.

This is why we started our accountability groups in the 7 Figure Runway and 7 Figure Altitude masterminds. During these meetings, we all talk about our specific goals, such as to negotiate 50 deals, flip 10 houses, or start building out our teams. Soon we realized that to accomplish these lengthy, complicated goals, we'd have to break them down into smaller chunks. You don't simply decide to hire an acquisitions manager or dramatically increase volume and achieve that goal the next day. Small, incremental steps forward are the only way to consistently meet and exceed big goals. Consistent action separates big-time investors from dabblers.

But to take that action week after week—especially when results are slow to come—we all need to support each other. And for those who have no trouble setting goals but are often distracted by the next big thing, accountability groups can act as a reset button.

We also realized that each of us benefited from being in a community of people who wanted us to succeed.

Andy Cepeda told his accountability group that his first goal was to get one contract. After succeeding, he told the group that next time he'd get three. But after five weeks without another contract, and the demands of his regular job taking a toll, Andy confessed that he wasn't going to make it.

"Guys, there's no way I can get three contracts this quarter."

Andy's big problem, and the main reason he needed the accountability group, was that his job made it virtually impossible to follow up with leads during normal business hours. And as you've learned, many wholesale deals come to fruition only because of diligent follow-up.

But the group encouraged Andy to stick with it, and in Week 8, he managed to get two contracts in a single week.

Ashly Whitaker was committed to getting her bookkeeping under control. After telling her group that a big project had come up that needed her attention, everyone supported her decision to take a three-week detour.

But in Week 4, the group asked, "Ashly, can you get your bookkeeping back on track this week?"

As entrepreneurs, we tend to downplay how much time and effort it takes to finish a project. What Ashly thought would take a few hours actually took 14. If her accountability group hadn't reminded her of her commitment, she could have had a serious problem on her hands a few months later.

Of course, these groups aren't just helpful when you're struggling or just starting out. Jimmey Green's business was going pretty well when he joined. But once members begin to turn a profit, they often forget to continue to invest time and money into leads. When Jimmey told his group he had stopped marketing, they immediately helped him understand why he needed to get it up and running again ASAP.

This is the path that will take you from learning to action. Your success depends on goals and accountability. Set your goals, find someone to hold you accountable, and you'll be blown away by what you're able to get done over the next 12 months.

> **FLIGHT PLAN HANDBOOK:**
> **Set Your Goals**
>
> Consider where you want to be 30, 60, 90, and 365 days from today. If you aren't ready to make concrete goals at the one-year mark yet, that's okay. Focus on the short term for now.
>
> For a printable worksheet to help you craft a SMART goal, check out your Flight Plan Handbook at 7FFHandbook.com..

I encourage you to set big goals and take big strides. Shoot high. Be bold. But I also hope that you reach out to others to help you achieve them. From where I am today, it's never been more clear to me that I needed to learn from others to accelerate my success. Between becoming familiar with all the processes and steps—not to mention the legal stuff and paperwork, networking with lenders and other investors, and learning how to lead a team—this business can take a lifetime to get right.

But it doesn't have to.

Don't Go It Alone

Just 12 houses—that was all I needed.

I figured if I could flip a dozen houses and make $30,000 profit on each, that extra income of $360,000 for the year would set me up for whatever I wanted to do next.

It would give me the time and freedom I wanted. It would pay for a good home for my family and allow us to travel. It would give my wife the option of flying to England to visit her parents whenever she wanted.

Twelve houses. One flip per month. It seemed reasonable.

There was just one problem—I had never flipped a house in less than six months. And that was with me spending all my evenings and weekends working on them.

I had spent months finding the houses. Then I had spent weeks navigating the purchase process. I had spent months renovating them and dealing with contractors who never seemed to show up on time or stick to the budget. Finally, I had spent weeks trying to sell the houses after finishing the repairs.

These two projects ate up all of my focus and all of my free time. And they'd still taken way longer than my goal. I needed to figure out a better way to do it.

A few days after selling my second flip, I got up at 5:00 AM to run a couple miles before heading down to the base. I grabbed my phone and my earbuds and set out in the dark.

It was October and still warm in northern Florida. Autumn comes late to that part of the country, if it comes at all. I made my way through quiet streets and flipped through a few podcasts on my phone as I ran.

About halfway through my route, I pulled up a podcast episode about something called 7 Figure Flipping. The podcast was hosted by a guy named Justin Williams, who had figured out how to flip 100+ houses per year in southern California while working just a few hours per week.

I wasn't totally sure I believed him. But I'd listened to a few of his previous episodes and he always had good insights. He seemed trustworthy.

Turns out 7 Figure Flipping was a mastermind group he had just launched for serious, experienced real estate investors. The idea was simple—meet up with other investors a few times per year, share what's working and what's not working, network, learn, and grow.

I listened. I thought about it.

That afternoon, I called Justin and asked if I could join.

Three months later, I found myself sitting at a conference table in a small hotel on a cold morning in Dana Point, California. Also sitting around that table were 20 other real estate investors. None of us had met before, but we had all come for the same reason.

We had come because we felt completely alone and had no one to turn to who understood what we were going through or the dreams we were chasing.

Most of us were house flippers and wholesalers. Some of us owned rentals. A few of us had done a couple development deals. Some were lenders or had worked as agents in the past. That table was like a scaled-down version of the entire real estate ecosystem brought together in one room.

Justin Williams stood, smiled, and greeted everyone. "Welcome to the first 7 Figure Flipping mastermind meeting." He was a former college football player, a churchgoer, a Boy Scout leader, a husband, and a father. The most wholesome all-American guy imaginable.

"I've never done anything like this before," he said. "But with the right people in the right room, we can all learn from each other. That's why we're here."

It was the start of something groundbreaking.

This group put me on the path to doing 200 deals per year.

Over the next 12 months, I met with the 7 Figure Flipping mastermind four times. I sat down with investors who were already doing 10+ deals per month, and they showed me the exact steps they had taken to get there.

I found out their best deal sources.

I learned their negotiation tactics—what to say and what *not* to say.

I used their contracts and documents.

I copied their marketing strategies.

I "borrowed" their hiring and training guides.

I followed their funding formulas.

I tapped into their lenders, mail houses, title companies, and other vendors.

I signed up for the exact tools and systems they used.

I studied their organizational structures.

They walked me through all of it. I didn't figure this stuff out on my own. (And neither had they.)

I hacked what was already working. And when I ran into walls, I looked around and saw a couple dozen other people who had already hit those same ones and figured it out. Seeing that gave me the strength to keep going.

I did a lot more than 12 deals that year and made a lot more than $360,000.

As my business grew, I started coaching some of the newer investors in the group. Then I joined 7 Figure Flipping as the COO, helping Justin run events and manage what was now a community of more than 150 high-level mastermind members.

In June of 2019, Justin came to me with a crazy idea. "Hey, man. You interested in taking over the company?"

That's how I ended up running 7 Figure Flipping.

And I'm proud to say that 7 Figure Flipping has grown into one of the leading real estate investor training organizations in the nation.

No successful investor, including myself, got there on their own. The real estate ecosystem isn't just interconnected businesses—it's interconnected *people*. People working together. People sharing their systems and strategies. People lifting each other up and giving encouragement when life gets hard.

Don't try to do this alone. Find your tribe, plug in, learn from them, and when you're ready, look for ways to give back. The results are more than worth it.

I wish you all the best on your real estate journey.

For more training, events, mentoring, and other resources, head over to 7FigureFlipping.com

Can't wait to see what you accomplish!

Acknowledgements

Writing a book was a goal of mine ever since I saw my dad's name in the World Book Encyclopedia. Without his guidance, there is no way I would be where I am today or the man you see now.

I'm eternally grateful to my wife—who has been by my side and my biggest supporter—from the early stages of being property rich and very cash poor to building a business to finding financial freedom on the other side. Thank you for everything, Lucy!

To my three little boys, I hope this book serves to remind you to always follow your dreams, no matter how ambitious other people may say you are. You can do whatever you want in this world, the possibilities are endless!

A very special thanks to my mentors Justin, Andy, and Mike. Without you guys, I never would have known this business was possible at the level I am operating at now. You drew the map for me to follow, thank you for allowing me to copy off of your homework!

To all of our 7 Figure Runway and Altitude members, your impact in my life through this mastermind group has been amazing. Thank you for voting with your dollars and believing in yourself (and us) to make the commitment to change your business and your life. I have learned so much from you all.

Finally, to the whole team at 7 Figure Flipping and Blackjack Real Estate thank you. My success is our success and it always will be, whether we are still working together or you have moved on to do other things yourself I will never forget the role you played in my life!

About The Author

Bill Allen, a Navy pilot and real estate professional, is the CEO and owner of 7 Figure Flipping and host of the 7 Figure Flipping Podcast, where he leads the top house flipping and wholesaling mentoring groups in the world. Just a few years ago, he was stuck flipping one or two houses per year and doing all the work himself. But since then, he's built a systematized business that runs without him. His wholesaling and flipping company Blackjack Real Estate does upwards of 200 deals a year.

In 2007, as an accidental landlord, Bill fell into real estate investing when he was deployed overseas and forced to leave his primary residence in San Diego. He continued to buy rentals at each duty station after that. Upon his return from abroad, and with marriage and kids in his future, Bill worked on a plan to fully retire in his early forties. His rental portfolio was growing, but he was running out of money quicker than he was building passive income. To build the capital required to purchase more rentals, Bill turned to house flipping.

In 2015, Bill founded Blackjack Real Estate, LLC with the mission of helping homeowners sell their houses for cash. The company started in Pensacola, Florida, and over time has expanded to Chattanooga and Nashville. Based out of Nashville, Bill and his team currently flip and wholesale almost 200 deals per year. What began as a one-man operation has quickly become a team of 15+ who are experts in their fields and passionate about real estate and helping others.

About 7 Figure Flipping

7 Figure Flipping is a community of impact-driven real estate investors who relentlessly pursue success and are called to help others do the same. We help house flippers and wholesalers do more deals, make more money, work fewer hours, and spend more time focused on what they REALLY want in life—whether that's making memories with their loved ones, giving back to their communities, building a legacy to pass on to their children, or something else.

This is what freedom looks like. This is what's possible through real estate investing.

This book only scratches the surface of how to get there. I wrote this as a starting point. Now that you understand the basics, you're ready to dive deeper into the systems and processes that real investors are using today to flip and wholesale 100's of houses per year.

My team and I run two mastermind groups to help real estate investors reach their freedom goals.

- **7 Figure Altitude:** A curated community of experienced investors who are ready to dig into topics like scaling, hiring a team, automating their operations, and removing themselves from the day-to-day hustle while doing more deals and increasing their income.
- **7 Figure Runway:** A 12-month "roadmap" program for new-to-intermediate investors who are ready to follow a proven process to launch and grow a house flipping or wholesaling business from the ground up as fast as possible.

Both of these groups are built around a core of accountability, authentic relationships, abundance, and the kind of personal support and encouragement you can only get from other investors who understand what you're going through and why you're doing it.

This is where you'll find your people—the people who "get it."

It's like coming home.

If you're ready to take the next step, I'd like to invite you to join us in one of these groups—whichever one is right for you and your journey.

It starts with a quick application.

- **Experienced Investors:** Apply to join 7 Figure Altitude at 7FigureAltitude.com.
- **New Investors:** Apply to join 7 Figure Runway and 7FigureRunway.com.

Why do we require an application? In short, we are fiercely committed to protecting the integrity of these two communities. Our members are like family. We share openly, talk about our struggles, and get vulnerable with each other. If there's even one "toxic" person in the room—someone who's a "taker" and not a giver—all of that connection and accountability and authenticity disappears. That's why we work hard to attract investors who share our core values of extreme ownership, stewardship, hard work, integrity, and personal / professional development. No complainers allowed.

You are the average of the five people you spend the most time with… and these groups are how you get around the RIGHT people.

Whether you're brand new to investing or you want to scale your already-profitable business, I encourage you to fill out an application. My team will personally guide you to the resource that is right for you. Think of it as a free consultation to help you nail down the next step in your journey—whether it involves joining one of our groups or not.

Inside the 7 Figure Flipping community, our members will show you what's working. They'll support you when you need it. We pick each other up, offer advice, and work together to reach our own personal freedom goals.

7 Figure Flipping is the #1 resource for serious investors who want to build thriving, consistent, profitable businesses flipping and wholesaling houses.

- You'll learn how to flip and wholesale houses at scale, without seeing any of the properties or using any of your own money, in ANY market.
- You'll learn the marketing strategies and deal sources that are working RIGHT NOW, in TODAY'S market.
- You'll build lifelong relationships with other committed investors who will inspire and encourage you and help you when things get rough.

The only question is... are YOU ready to grow your income and your impact?

Learn more at 7FigureFlipping.com... or dive in headfirst and apply to join 7 Figure Altitude or 7 Figure Runway at the links above. (And, if you haven't already, go check out 7FFHandbook.com for access to YOUR Flight Plan Handbook.)

I'll see you around!